MW00458779

Journey of a Lifetime

David Tipton

Copyright © 2020 David Tipton
All rights reserved.
ISBN: 9781706218661

Book Cover Designed by:
FAITHWORKS Image Consulting

DEDICATION

I am so happy to be able to dedicate this book to mine and my wife's parents.

David and Faye Tipton
Bill and Goldie Hayes

Memories are so special to me!
Mom and Dad – Thanks for the memories!

Table of Contents

ACKNOWLEDGEMENTS

The first person that I ever heard say this was the late Senator from North Carolina, Jessie Helms – "When you see a turtle on top of a fence post, chances are, he did not get there on his own." I think I am safe to say that it is impossible for a turtle to reach the top of a fence post on its own. It's lucky if it gets across the highway.

When I think about all the people in my life who have helped me, the list is way too long to put on a single page. I am a composite of everyone who has touched my life in some way or another. Although, I wrote alone, I certainly did not write this manuscript alone.

Parents, pastors, mentors, advisors, relatives, teachers, friends and yes, adversaries, have knowingly or unknowingly had a role in helping me write this book of stories, lessons and recollections which have been in my heart for several years.

SPECIAL THANKS

First and foremost, I give God all of the glory and honor. Without Him, I am like a ship without a sail.

Secondly, to my dear wife: She's got style, she's got grace, and she's a winner. She's a lady. While your childhood took place in Paragould, Arkansas and mine took place in Port St. Joe, Florida – even then God knew that we were _meant_ to be.

To my executive secretary, Kristina Osborne: Thank you falls way too short for the countless hours you have put in to help me achieve this dream. I am especially grateful for your editorial help.

Lastly, Dan Gwaltney, who gave me the sermon idea that Adam Had No Childhood.

Jonathan Tipton
Born: 1659
Died: 1757

Jonathan Tipton
Born: 1699
Died: ?

William Tipton
Born: 1736
Died: 1798

Thomas Tipton
Born: 1762
Died: 1830

Rev. Benjamin Tipton
Born: 1804
Died: 1878

*

Jason Vander Tipton
Born: Aug 31, 1832
Died: Jan 21, 1891

Chatman Bostick Tipton
Born: Mar 20, 1871
Died: May 3, 1944

Charlie Harold Tipton, Sr.
Born: Feb 28, 1906
Died: Jan 3, 1981

David Devonn Tipton, Sr.
Born: July 19, 1932
Died: Aug 4, 2004

m.
3/11/1978

David Devonn Tipton, Jr.
Born: January 17, 1957

Gwenda Hayes Tipton
Born: January 30, 1956

Damon Tipton
Born: March 7, 1982

David Devonn Tipton, III
Born: March 28, 1980

Kanon and Kade Tipton
Born: Oct 4, 2006, Dec 2, 2009

Cooper Tipton
Born: June 10, 2009

The Tipton Family
Genealogy
1659 - 2020

David and Gwen Tipton

The Tipton
Grandchildren

Anna Kate Tipton
4/30/2010

Kade Tipton
12/2/2009

Kamdon Andrus
3/8/2009

Cooper Tipton
6/10/2008

Kanon Tipton
10/4/2006

McKayla Bailey
8/1/2005

Ellie Grace Woods
9/1/2020

Liam Weaver
10/24/2016

Presley Woods
5/31/2015

Kate Weaver
5/10/2015

Darlynn Grace Tipton
12/5/2012

Ava Claire Tipton
12/2/2012

Brantley Woods
8/21/2012

11

PREFACE

How many times have you pulled off the highway at a historical marker to reflect on a site's place in history? Probably not often. We are always in a hurry. I can hear my sons, Devonn and Damon now, "Dad, do we have to stop at *every* historical marker?" As children on vacation with their parents, their only interest was to get to our destination as soon as possible. They wanted to get in every second they could to ride the roller coaster and race each other on the go-karts before dad had to announce way too soon, "Okay, it's time to go home."

I realize that not everyone will want to stop by and visit some of my historical markers. However, while traveling down the road to your own destination, you may happen to pass by and take a quick glance at mine, and perhaps I will provoke you to pay close attention to your own personal "historical markers." God-centered reflection benefits us and our families. That is why admonitions to pass on our testimonies and stories about God dot the Psalms. "*We will tell the next generation the praiseworthy deeds of the Lord, his power, and the wonders he has done.*" (Psalm 78:4).

From this mindset, I approach this book with the determination to share the goodness of God and His miraculous works in a way that only I can tell by nature of my experiences.

A few years ago, I was sitting in a class taught by my friend, Stanley Thrift. It was about personality types; I discovered that I am predominately sanguine. I was getting sort of puffed up with a little pride as he started speaking of the attributes and strengths of the sanguine. *Incredible*, I thought and remembered how Woody Woodpecker felt as he was pecking on a gigantic redwood when lightning hit it, and the tree split right down the middle. He leaned backwards, looked at the effects of his pecking, and said, "Whew, I'm good, but I didn't know that I was *that* good!"

All of this ran through my mind, only to have Stanley start meddlin', as we say. He began to speak on all of the weaknesses of sanguine people. Did he ever turn my hot water to a cold drip!

One of the weaknesses of a sanguine is that we talk too much. Stanley said a sanguine would take you around the world explaining something when many times a simple *yes* or *no* would have been sufficient. I often tell people that I talk so much that my tongue is sunburned – a little exaggerated, but correctly illustrated.

Another thing mentioned was those sanguine personalities tend to have bizarre things happen to them. *Wow,* I thought to myself as I studied Stanley, *this guy knows me better than I thought!* Truly, I have witnessed some bizarre things in my lifetime.

It would take a much larger book than this one to share the many unusual things that seem to be attracted to me. Some are humorous; others, sad. Many are undeniably miraculous. However in each of them, regardless of which way my emotional pendulum swings, there is a lesson taught and memories created.

As I write even now, I feel like I have entered an amusement park and I'm standing in line to ride the roller coaster, knowing that once I get on the ride, there will be ups and downs and a few unexpected curves thrown into my path. I know that it doesn't make sense to bail out, so I'll just hang on, stay put and enjoy the ride because it will all be over after a while. And when it is time to exit and I look back over my shoulder, I want to be able to say, "Man, what a ride!"

"Life is a rush into the unknown. You can duck down and hope nothing hits you, show your teeth, and say dish it up

baby, and don't be stingy with the jalapenos." (Fireman Funds advertisement)

David Tipton

Chapter One

Adam Had No Childhood

*"And not only so, but we glory in tribulations also: knowing that tribulation worketh patience; And patience, **experience**, and **experience**, hope"*

Romans 5:3-4

God created Adam with perfect knowledge. Adam's first tasks reflect this natural wisdom. When God brought all the living creatures to Adam to see what he would name each of them, the names he gave them seem to suggest that he had a knowledge of things already within him. For example, he called Eve *Woman*, for "she was taken out of man," (Genesis 2:23). This indicates Adam had a logical reason for calling her *Woman* based on God-given knowledge since he had never been to school or had any formal education.

Just think – a *real* know it all!

Adam never spent time studying or doing homework. He already knew everything he needed to know. He did not have to chase a school bus because he overslept or listen to teachers teach the folly of evolution. He never experienced falling from a bicycle and scraping his knee or the pains of puppy love. He had no security system installed in the garden for fear of intruders. There was no one to intrude! He had no microwave or dishes to wash since God prepared his meals. April 15th would have been the same as any other day to Adam since he had no forms to fill out or taxes to pay.

Yes, Adam really had it made. God made him a wife of his own rib. He did not have to date Eve, take her to dinner and spend enormous amounts of time and money trying to "sway her" into seeing him as Prince Charming. He did not have to **experience** any of that.

Men think of this: He never had to go shopping with her!

Adam had no friends to criticize him or to borrow things from him and never return them. He never had to compete to get in a conversation with others because there were no others.

The problem with Adam was that he had no childhood, and as a result, he had no **experience**.

David said, "*I have never seen the righteous forsaken nor his seed begging bread,*" (Psalm 37:25). This was **experience** talking, not just knowledge. He was able to confidently take on and slay the Philistine giant based on his previous **experience** of killing a bear and a lion. When the bear and lion came upon his flock, he had to make some life and death decisions. If he ran, the sheep would die, but he would likely live. If he stayed and fought the bear, he could have been killed. His victory, through having **experienced** the delivering hand of God in both of these traumatic events, gave him the courage and strength to trust God to deliver the giant into his hands also. Therefore, he had the courage to proclaim, "*Who is this uncircumcised Philistine that he should defy the armies of the Living God?*" (I Samuel 17:26). David had tremendous confidence in God because of his prior **experiences** where God had shown His great love and strength.

Paper qualifications are no substitute for real life **experience**!

I believe that there is power in prayer, and it's not because I have a degree from a theological institute, and not just because the Bible says there is. I have **experienced** the miraculous for myself.

The Historical Marker

This historical marker is perhaps my first memory and eyewitness of the power of prayer. My mother faithfully knelt with her children every night before retiring for the evening. We would recite her version of "Now I lay me down to sleep." On this particular night I recollect, we needed more than a recital of a memorized prayer. The circumstances surrounding this family dilemma left an indelible stamp on my heart, and perhaps this experience was one of the reasons that led me to be a follower of Jesus Christ beginning at an early age.

As I recall, I was barely five years old. My siblings, Steve, Ricky, and Debbie were four, three, and one, respectively. My youngest brother Ricky was a free bleeder, and without warning on numerous occasions, both of Ricky's nasal passages would begin to bleed profusely. Prior to this, Mother was able to stop the bleeding and things would return to normal. On this night, everything Mother tried, failed. She was bathing my brother in ice cold water and had already filled one towel with blood and was using the second towel.

I vividly remember hearing Mother call out to Steve and me, "Boys, come here. Mommy needs you."

We had no vehicle, no telephone and now, Mom was asking Steve and me to start praying. She said, "I need you to help Mommy pray, and let's ask God to send Daddy home. We need Daddy to come home now."

We began to pray, "God, send Daddy home. God, Mom needs Daddy to come home now!"

In the meantime, my dad was in a nearby town leaving a bar with the intention of driving over to a neighboring city to go to another bar. While driving our only family car, a 1956 Chevrolet, in the opposite direction of our house, the generator light began to blink. Not wanting to be stranded on the highway, Dad thought to himself, *Hmmm, I better turn around and go home.*

He did a U-turn to come home, and the generator light stopped blinking. He began to think it must have been a short or a bad connection. So, he turned around again to go to the bar, only to look down and see that little red light blinking again. There are moments in time when God can use something as little as a generator light to alter an entire family. Three times the light blinking scenario happened, and each time Dad would turn around. After the third time, he said to himself, *Faye and the kids must need me. I'm going home.*

I can still remember the feeling of exhilaration and victory as we heard a call pull into the driveway. We rushed to the window to discover the headlights of our 1956 Chevrolet in front of our house, and on the steps was the man that we were asking God to send home.

My dad stepped into the door and quickly realized that there was a family emergency. He scooped up my little brother and loaded his family into the car – that no longer had a blinking generator light. With all the fervency you can imagine in such a situation, we rushed to the hospital in the city.

After the emergency was taken care of and everything began to settle down, Daddy shared the story of the blinking light. I learned that night God hears even a child's prayer and it could be the generator for a miracle that ultimately God uses as an alternator of individuals and families' lives.

Be encouraged friend! Who else would enjoy hearing this story today?

Chapter Two

Window Shopping

"And the Lord God called unto Adam, and said unto him, where are thou?"

Genesis 3:9

"Saying where is he that is born King of the Jews…?"
Matthew 2:2

Upon reading the first question in the Old Testament and the first question in the New Testament, we obviously see a disconnect between God and man. In the Old Testament, it is God looking for man. In the New Testament, it is man looking for God.

For six dispensations, God deals with mankind in a certain way. When it was all said and done, there was still a missing piece to the puzzle of redemption that would connect God to man and man to God. There was a chasm, a disconnect. The bridge was out.

Michelangelo depicted this feeling in his painting on the ceiling of the Sistine Chapel in Vatican City. In this huge fresco painting of creation, God's right arm is outstretched toward man's left arm. Famously, Adam's finger and God's finger are separated by a slight distance.

That same scenario is evident when we pay a visit to the Arlington Cemetery of the Bible in Hebrews the eleventh chapter. Fourteen times, the Scripture says, *"By faith,"* and three times it says, *"through faith"* as it describes the victors and the victims of faith. Verse thirteen says, *"These all died in faith, not having received the promises, but having seen them afar off, and were persuaded of them, and embraced them, and confessed that they were strangers and pilgrims on the earth."* Subsequently in verses thirty-nine and forty, the chapter concludes by saying, *"And these all, having obtained a good report through faith, received not the promise: God having provided some better thing for us, that they without us should not be made perfect."*

Then Peter chimed in, *"Unto whom it was revealed, that not unto themselves, but unto us they did minister the things, which are now reported unto you by them that have preached the gospel unto you with the Holy Ghost sent down from heaven; which things the angels desire to look into."* (I Peter 1:12).

It is as if the heroes in Hebrews 11 and the angels are all window shopping.

One of my fondest memories and experiences of childhood occurred when Dad or Mom would say, "Does anyone want to go window shopping?"

Of course, the vote was unanimous. So, we would load up in the car and drive to town. Dad would park the car in the parking lot of the St. Joseph Telephone and Telegraph Company on the north end of Reid Avenue in Port St. Joe, Florida. These were the days before supercenters or shopping malls, when the businesses on Main Street would close at 4:30 PM. Our family would start out walking on the west side of the street, walk all the way down to the end of the street, and come back up on the east side of Reid Avenue. We would peer in every window and fantasize about having all this merchandise.

My brothers and I would argue as we looked in the window of Mr. David May's Western Auto. The condensation would form as we cupped our hands around our faces, breathed on the window, and laid claim to the Western Flyer bicycle with dual headlights and streamers hanging from the handlebars. Steve would say, "That one over there is mine!" and then Ricky would say, "No, it's not, it's mine!" Then I would chime in and say, "No way, I claimed it first!" Then we would all cry in a frenzy of voices, "Mom! Dad! Tell them that's my bicycle! I said it first!"

In reality, it didn't belong to any of us. The store was closed, the owner had gone home, and we were simply window shopping.

At one time in my childhood, I had been eyeing a sunburst guitar in the picture window of the Philco Store and wishing that it were mine. I recall the Friday evening that we stopped in front of the Philco Store and I said out loud, "Man, I wish

Reid Avenue – Port St. Joe,

I had that guitar, but I don't have enough money." I shined shoes at Mr. Jack Hammock's barbershop and had saved up $12.00. That's a lot of money to a nine-year-old boy charging fifty-cents for a shoeshine and made sure to give God His ten percent plus a dollar a week to the campground fund.

After hearing me say, "Man, I wish I had enough money to buy that guitar," my Dad said, "Son, if you have worked that hard to save twelve dollars, then Dad will make up the difference, and you can come here Monday and buy that guitar if you want it."

Wow! I will never forget how excited I was when I walked in there on Monday and said to the owner, "Sir, I'd like to buy that guitar over there in the window." I had finally gone beyond window shopping to actually getting into the store. He reached up to the guitar and handed it down to me. I captured a picture in my mind which stays with me to this very day, as he hit the large keys of that huge NCR (National Cash Register). In large numeric tabs it read, $20.60. I walked out embracing something that I had wanted for a long time.

This reminds me of a time the disciples went fishing. They fished all night with no results. Seldom do men fish and catch nothing – but when they do, like my dad did, God shows up early and makes up the difference.

Up until the Day of Pentecost found in the first two chapters in the Book of Acts, all of the preceding generations could do nothing but window shop. They desired and longed for a better way and a better promise. They searched for better things to come. The owner opened the store and said, "*Whosoever will, let him come…*"

It happened when Peter, who had the keys, stood that day and preached the inaugural message of salvation. He preached about David's very own window shopping **experiences** in verses 25 and 31 of Acts 2: "*For David speaketh concerning him, I foresaw the Lord always before my face… He seeing this before spake of the resurrection…*"

I find it ironic that the 39th verse of Hebrews 11 said, "*And these all, having obtained a good report through faith, received not the promise.*" And the 39th verse of Acts chapter 2 says, "*For the promise is unto you, and to your children, and to all that are a far off, even as many as the Lord our God shall call.*"

My friend, you no longer have to stand on the outside looking through the window saying wistfully, "I sure wish I could have what's on the inside." The door is open! Come on in! Daddy has already paid the price.

Be encouraged friend! Who else would enjoy hearing this story today?

Chapter Three

Roots of My Raising

I cannot help but think about the words to the old country
song recorded by Merle Haggard:

I left the four-lane highway
Took a blacktop seven miles
Down by the old country school
I went to as a child
Two miles down a gravel road I could see
The proud old home
A tribute to a way of life
That's almost come and gone

The roots of my raising run deep
I come back for the strength that I need
And hope comes no matter how far down I sink
The roots of my raising run deep.

As a young lady with four small children, my mother
began to pray that God would help her find the Truth and the
right church to bring her children up in. It is amazing to me
how God orchestrated events and circumstances to introduce
us to the saving message of the Gospel.

Looking down the old dusty roads of my life, I can clearly
see the hand of God on our family; He ordered our steps.

Just a few weeks shy of my sixth birthday on December
27, 1962, God filled my mother with His Spirit. I remember
like it was yesterday. I was a child. My dad was outside the
church with me and my siblings. He would lift each of us up
to see through the window, as my mom was lost in the Spirit.
This revolutionized our family, and this is where I began to

love the ministry and learn the value of having a pastor in my life.

Pastor and Sister Gordon Adams with Tipton Siblings

My first shepherd was Pastor Gordon Adams. He would strap on his Gibson guitar just before he would preach and stir my soul, while singing songs like, "Take this message to my mother" and "If I could hear my mother pray again." Pastor Adams would tell the story of how he ran away from home at sixteen, joined the army and never saw his mother again. But he knew her prayers eventually reached his heart. He became an Apostolic preacher and started a church in Wewahitchka, Florida, the church that God led my mother and her children to be a part of.

The first chapter of this book speaks to the fact that Adam had no childhood. So, that means he didn't have a Sunday School teacher, a church to attend or a pastor to preach Truth to him. I learned through experience early on of the importance of having a man of God in my life.

I recall one day in elementary school, all the boys in my class were playing flag football during Physical Education class. For some reason, just before we were getting ready for the next play, my classmates began to ostracize and make fun of my religion. To this day, I do not know what sparked this painful conversation. However, while they were calling me a Holy Roller, etc., I felt the heat and verbal jabs and blurted out, "I don't know what you are talking about. I'm not a Holy Roller! I don't know Jesus!" The moment I said that, it was as though the venetian blind over the window of my heart closed. Great fear came over me and for the next two or three weeks, a dark cloud hung over my mind and my heart. I thought I had blasphemed the Holy Ghost. Satan was tormenting my mind.

One Sunday night I was coming out of the prayer room, walking toward the sanctuary. I passed by the doorway to the small Sunday School office where my pastor stood.

He called me by name and said, "Step in here for a minute. Brother Adams would like to speak to you." He politely asked me, "Now what's wrong with you?" I replied, "Nothing, Brother Adams." He said, "Yes, there is. Your worship has fallen off, and you seem uptight. Now, tell me what's going on?" I immediately burst into tears and began sobbing uncontrollably. With a broken heart, I began to say to him, "I've denied Jesus in front of my classmates. I've blasphemed the Holy Ghost!" I told him exactly what had happened on the playground that day.

He looked at me and said, "Here is what I want you to do. Start praying and ask God to forgive you for what you have done."

I began to pray aloud and ask God to forgive me and be merciful. Then he stopped me from praying and assured me that God had heard my prayer and that I was forgiven. Then he said, "Now, dry your tears, go out there and take your seat and start worshipping God like you are supposed to." Thank God for a pastor! We later moved to Panama City, Florida, where we attended the Apostolic Pentecostal Church located in St. Andrews, Florida, pastored by C.F. Anderson. He instilled in me a love for Truth and a commitment to following the Word of God with all my heart. I still remember the words of wisdom that he shared with me. Things like… "Don't toot your own horn, turn your headlights on." Later in my mid-twenties, I went to him one day to discuss that I felt a call to preach. He asked me a few pertinent questions and imparted some words of wisdom.

For two years, he never mentioned a word to me about preaching. Frankly, I thought he had forgotten we even had the discussion. I never spoke to anyone about it. Then out of the blue, one Sunday night after service, he called me to the platform. He informed me that he had to be out of town the following week and that I would be preaching the mid-week service. He apologized that he would not be there to hear my first message. I studied and prayed for the next three days and preached my first message from Hebrews 11 entitled, "Seeing the invisible." I read my text, announced my title, and wrapped it up in about five minutes due to being so nervous and running out of things to say. I don't think that has happened since. Some say, I don't know when to quit.

Yes, the roots of my raising run deep. They have sustained me even through the most difficult storms of life and led me on a journey from that independent church to the United Pentecostal Church. I still remember the day I was invited to join this great organization. I got in my car and drove eight hours to visit with my pastor, Brother Anderson.

I told him I had been asked to join the United Pentecostal Church, and I wanted his wisdom and blessing. He replied, "Son, the United Pentecostal Church offers more opportunities to minister than any other Apostolic organization that I know of. Always stay true to what you know and what you believe, and you will do fine."

I have followed those words of wisdom with all of my heart. All these years later, I still believe this great organization offers the best opportunity to minister and impact the world. I have remained true to what I believe and know to be true. God has blessed, and I have seen great and mighty things done for the Kingdom.

Pastor Anderson and I

Be encouraged friend! Who else would enjoy hearing this story today?

Chapter Four

Dismantle the Silo

"For none of us lives to himself, and no one dies to himself."
Romans 14:7, NJKV

"All mankind is one author, and is one volume; when one man dies, one chapter is not torn out of the book, but translated into a better language; and every chapter must be so translated... As therefore the bell that rings to a sermon, calls not upon the preacher only, but upon the congregation to come: so this bell call us all: but how much more me, who am brought so near the door by this sickness... <u>No man is an island, entire of itself, every man is a piece of the continent, a piece of the main...</u>"

(John Donne)

"Many hands make light work."

(John Heywood)

At 17 years of age, I moved to West Point, Mississippi. Mr. Wyliss Kemp, Store Owner of Sunflower #67 hired me as Produce Manager. Mr. Kemp taught me much about customer service and that the "customer is always right." He almost convinced me that the phrase "Cleanliness is next to Godliness" was in the Holy Writ. He believed in keeping the shelves cleaned and stocked. The years he dealt with the public set a good example for me in developing leadership skills.

In 1974, I moved from Panama to West Point. While there, I stayed as often as I could with the Higginbotham's. They are even to this day just like my family. Brother Joe worked for one of the Bryan Brother's Farms. I will always cherish memories of hauling hay, riding horses, tending cows and enjoying Sister Higginbotham's cooking.

Looking back, there were so many things that I learned on the farm. Things I would have never received from Rutherford High School in Panama City, Florida, where I attended. One intriguing item is the silo – that tall, cylindrical structure in which fodder is stored. It holds complex mixtures of grains and other nutrients that generate chemical reactions in the feed, maintaining the herd's health and level of milk production. Yet, because the silo's airtight walls cut off ventilation, they also exude toxic fumes. If the chemistry goes wrong, the chemical reaction can contaminate that same feed.

By the same token, an individual, church, district, or organization, by limiting its air intake to its own work or doesn't recognize that its reactions can affect the whole system, its deliberations could be dangerous to itself and others.

Current headlines and recent news stories make it clear that pressing issues are too big for silo thinking. Each of us face hefty agendas these days; we cannot afford to engage in "silo thinking." Searching for innovative ways to share ideas and resources, can break down institutional barriers, making it easier for a young couple to go and start a church. Now is the time to assemble teams that crisscross other committees mixed with elders and young preachers for an effective shared governance.

With shared responsibilities, the workload is distributed, the decision-making will be cooperative, and the unique gifts of every minister in the Kingdom will be welcomed.

For shared governance to run smoothly, each group and every individual must respect the prerogatives of the others, while at the same time, holding each other accountable for the overall well-being of our churches and districts.

Let's not sell the farm; let's just dismantle the silos.

Be encouraged friend! Who else would enjoy hearing this story today?

Chapter Five

A Tribute to David Tipton, Sr.

"Honor thy father and mother, which is the first commandment with promise."

Ephesians 6:2

On July 19, 1932, my dad, David Devonn Tipton, was the second child born to Charlie Harold and Dora Viola O'Brian Tipton. He arrived at the onset of the great depression and experienced the difficulties of being a sharecropper's son. Dad's oldest brother, my Uncle Junior, shared this experience with me that I never knew, and it explained why Dad very seldom would wear a new shirt or pair of slacks that we gave him as a gift because he would say, "I'm saving these for hard times." As small barefooted boys, Dad and Uncle Junior were walking down a dirt road one day and were very hungry when my dad saw where someone had tossed an orange peeling on the side of the road. He ran over, picked it up and gave half to his brother. **That's the kind of man my dad was!**

As a young single man, Dad left Calhoun County, Florida, and moved to Port St. Joe, Florida. Mr. George Tapper, former Lieutenant Governor hired him as a construction worker. They built roads and bridges all around Newport, Sopchoppy and Perry, Florida. During this time, my mother was visiting her sister, my Aunt June. Dad came over to their house. When he walked in the living room, he looked at mom and said, "You are going to be my wife." Obviously, mom was taken back and embarrassed. Soon thereafter, he went to Mr. Tapper and said to him, "Mr. Tapper, I've found this girl that I want to marry. Can you help me get a job at the paper mill?"

Mr. Tapper made one phone call and without even filling out an application, Dad went to work on May 9, 1955, for the St. Joe Paper Company – a job that he loved and kept until he was forced to retire after forty-three years of dedicated and loyal service. By his example, Dad taught me never to be late for work and never bite the hand that feeds you. I have heard him say many times when someone complained about the foul odor coming out of the smokestack, "Smells like a paycheck to me." Many of his co-workers commented to me, during his funeral, that there was never a job too big for my dad. **That's the kind of man my dad was!**

St. Joe Paper Company

My poverty of words frustrates me, and time will not allow me to share all the fond memories I have. One such

memory recalls the time the entire family sat on the seawall eating popcorn and watching the sun go down on St. Joseph Bay. I recall Mom had saved up enough S&H Green stamps to redeem them for a plastic boat that would hold us four kids. Dad lit the Coleman lantern, and we kids got in the boat. He tied one end of a string to the bow of the boat and the other end to his belt loop and waded out into the bay with a gig – taking us "floundering" as we called it.

It was a highlight for us boys if Daddy said on Friday night before bed, "Boys, let's go to the car lots tomorrow." We have driven on trips of nearly a hundred-mile radius, from

St. Joe to Marianna on to Tallahassee, then to Panama City. We would jump out of our old car and find the one we wanted to test drive (knowing that we were not going to purchase one) and take it for a spin. We would get away from the dealership and say, "Daddy, see if it will spin the tires!" My dad is probably the reason that a salesman is now required to ride along on a test drive. **That's the kind of man my dad was!**

Daddy never wanted us to take up hunting and be around guns. He was so protective of us. Every morning as he was leaving the house for work, I can still hear him say, "Faye, now you watch them kids and don't let them get into anything."

However, we stayed on him about taking us deer hunting until he finally consented and borrowed a 410-shotgun. Early one Saturday morning, we "experienced" hunters headed for the woods to kill a deer. We left the main highway and went on into the country woods. Suddenly, Dad pulled the vehicle onto the shoulder of the road. We didn't know what he was doing. He let his window down, pointed the gun out the window at a crane and said, "Boys, you see that bird? Let me see if I can kill it." All three of us boys started crying and begging Daddy not to kill that cute bird. Dad said, "Boys, I can see right now that you don't want to go deer hunting." He unloaded the gun, rolled up the window and we went home. That was our first and last hunting trip with Dad. I think he knew exactly what he was doing. Dad was comical sometimes. **That's the kind of man my dad was!**

I will never forget one Saturday morning, Mom sent Dad to pay a bill and told him to get there before noon because they only stayed open a half day on Saturdays. She did explain to him that if he didn't manage to get there before noon, the business had a little slot at the bottom of the door gasket that he could simply slide the envelope under the door, and they would get it on Monday.

Well, you guessed it! It was after noon before he got there. So, he tried and tried to get the envelope under the door. He finally got his pocketknife to lift up the rubber seal, slid the envelope under the door, gave it a shove and watched it scoot about five feet or more into the business. At that moment, he looked up and there were several women who had been watching him all this time. It was then that it dawned on him. It was the wrong business. The *real* business was next door. So, he scrambled in the store on his knees, retrieved the envelope and left without saying a word.

Another humorous story among many comes to mind during the time my Dad carpooled to work from Panama City to Port St. Joe, which he did for several years. I recall on one occasion that Dad got up to go work, and we were out of deodorant. So, he reached in the medicine cabinet above the bathroom sink and got Mom's Avon Honeysuckle sachet, dabbed a little under each arm, and hurried off to work.

A few miles down the road, the driver of the vehicle commented, "Guys, I know you all are going to think I'm crazy, but it is in the middle of winter, and I am smelling honeysuckle!" Dad spoke up and said, "You know that's odd; I was about to say the same thing!" **That's the kind of many my dad was!**

In giving honor to my Dad, I also give honor to my Dad's wife, my mother. Mother was a faithful, loving, loyal wife to my dad. As a single man, Dad once made the statement. "I will never marry, but if I do, I want a wife who knows how to cook." I sincerely believe that if Dad had not married Mom, he would have never lived as long as he did. Mom took care of Dad not only by cooking well for him, but she also understood him more than anyone else in the world. When we kids couldn't figure him out, she understood him. He always wanted her nearby, and she stood with him through the good and the bad. Thanks, Mom!

Dad, you took care of us, and you never let us go hungry. You made sure that we were clothed, had a roof over our heads and had a vehicle for Mom to drive to church.

That's the kind of man my dad was! Dad, thanks for the memories!

My last mission in honoring my family is to point someone to God. Dad believed and would stand up for the plan of salvation and the message I preach.

If you are reading this today and you have never repented of your sins, been baptized in the precious Name of Jesus and received the gift of the Holy Ghost, I ask prayerfully that you would consider obeying Acts 2:38-39: *"Then Peter said unto them, Repent, and be baptized every one of you in the name of Jesus Christ for the remission of sins, and ye shall receive the gift of the Holy Ghost. For the promise is unto you, and to your children, and to all that are afar off, even as many as the Lord our God shall call."*

Tipton Family – 1966

***

The following tribute was given to my Dad in lieu of a customary Father's Day card on June 15, 2003.

Dear Dad,

Ephesians 6:2 commands us to *"honor your father and mother."* Since the day I wrote the tribute to Mom for last Mother's Day, I have been forming in my mind words of tribute to you, waiting for the right time to share them with you. Today is that day.

Much of what a man is and becomes arrives through his Dad, and as I scan the landscape of my heritage, my mind is racing as I think of all you have given me.

Thanks for working so hard on the same job for forty-three years when so many tried to get you to quit and try other things.

You taught me by example to be loyal to the Company (people) that you work for. You taught me to be punctual, to arrive early and stay late, and never bite the hand that feeds you.

Thanks for providing us with a vehicle so that we could go to church and for driving us to youth camp every year because you knew how important it was to us.

Thanks for the bicycles, toys and the surprises at Christmas. I know it must have been difficult to hide our Christmas gifts with us thinking that we were not going to get anything – somehow you managed to get it all the way to Augusta, Georgia, without us finding out about it. WOW, what memories!

Thanks for the hundreds of car lots we visited on Saturdays and for all the test drives of so many different cars, even though we knew we were not going to buy one. It sure was fun!

Thanks for helping me with my fifth-grade science project. You and one of your paper mill friends made a weathervane that we put outside Mrs. Betty Sue Anchor's classroom so that my entire class could look out the window and see which way the wind was blowing. And every time I looked out, I thought, "My dad made that."

How could I ever forget that every day when you would get out of Mr. Theodore Bishop's English Ford at the end of the street, we would run and hide behind the evergreen tree, and when you would pass by, we would jump out and scare you. Each time you would act like we scared you to death, and you knew we were there all along.

Thanks for wrestling with us. Remember how we would clear the living room floor, push aside the coffee table, and turn that room into an arena? We would all pile on you and then after we "whipped" you, we would pull the coffee table back into the center of the room. We four kids would climb up on top of the coffee table while you and Mom watched, and we would have our very own choir singing "Gathering Flowers for the Master's Bouquet" and many others.

Dad, I could write all day about the things you have given me, but I have to prepare a sermon for service tonight. I honor you, Dad, for you are worthy of double honor. I do not know, nor have I ever met, a man I would be more proud to call my father. So instead of a customary Father's Day card this year,

I wanted you to have this tribute from your namesake, David D. Tipton, Jr.

Your Son

Be encouraged friend! Who else would enjoy hearing this story today?

Chapter Six

The Short Bus

"For all have sinned and fall short of the glory of God."
Romans 3:23, NIV

Research confirms that everyone has unconscious or implicit bias – It's part of human nature. My experience told in this chapter is a unique way to help you focus on raising awareness of unconscious bias and steps you can take to prevent biased attitudes and behaviors that affect us at home, school, work and play. I believe awareness, understanding and a holistic approach to cultural sensitivities will go far in creating harmony in every environment.

Let me remind you, we are in this together! Let me illustrate a personal experience to make my point.

For several years I drove a school bus. That's the only time in life where your troubles are truly behind you. The last two years that I drove, I was a full-time substitute and never knew which route I would drive until I arrived that morning.

On one particular morning – the beginning of the third week of school – the fleet manager greeted me with his usual greeting and announced, "Well, today you're drivin' the handicap bus. By law, you've gotta have an assistant to help the children… and you." In most cases, the handicap bus is referred to as "the short bus". Herein lies the need for awareness in cultural sensitivities, especially among individuals with special needs in our society.

I went through the routine of firing up the bus, and we began to make our way around the county picking up handicapped children. Some were mentally handicapped; others were in wheelchairs and had physical impairments.

The assistant said to me, "Okay, this next stop is our last stop, and it's on the other side of town. But let me warn you now – one of those little boys has problems. He has epilepsy and has had a seizure every morning since school started while in route to school. We've had to turn around every morning and take him back home. He has not made it to school yet without issue."

So, we pulled up in front of the house and two cute little boys walked down the sidewalk. The assistant pointed to the one on the right and said, "That's him. He's the one that's got problems."

When the two boys stepped up on the bus, one took his seat and the assistant said to the other one, "You come here, *Josh, and sit here in front of me because you know you've got problems."

He took his seat and as I tugged the lever to pull the stop sign in and closed the door, she said to him again, "Now you sit right up there, and don't you go to sleep, because you know you've got problems."

I thought to myself, *oh no, I'm taking care of this situation. I'm not sure who it is that really has the problem. I am not going to let this person tell this kid he's got problems in front of all these other kids all the way to school until he has another seizure.*

So, I looked up in the broad mirror and said, "Hey kids, how many of you want to hear some jokes?"

All of them started jumping in their little wheelchairs and in their restrained seats. A chorus of excited voices cried, "Yes sir, Mr. Bus Driver, tell us some jokes!" So, I spent the next few minutes telling every joke that I could think of.

A wave of laughter erupted, and the children urged, "Tell us some more, Mr. Bus Driver."

I'll spare you all the jokes told to keep the assistant from reminding that boy he had problems, but there were quite a few. About halfway to school, I ran out of jokes. As we sat quietly at a red light, a long bus chugged to a stop alongside us.

Sensing the potential for an awkward moment, I said, "Hey kids, did you know that this bus has something that other buses do not have?"

Several heads craned around to get a look at me in the mirror over my head as I continued, "Oh, yeah! This bus has *hydraulics*."

Alternately, I dug my left foot into the brake and prodded the gas with my right foot, and the bus began to rock. All of a sudden, those handicapped kids begin to point their finger at the kids in the so-called normal bus and excitedly announce, "Goody! Goody! Our bus has hydraulics, and your bus doesn't!"

Then the light changed, I pressed the accelerator to the floor and leaped out ahead of the "long bus" and the children were so excited that we were outrunning the other bus. I realized once again that I was out of jokes. I searched my brain for ideas of what to do. Finally, I asked, "Hey, how many of you want me to sing?"

"Yes sir, Mr. Bus Driver, sing!" they consented.

Well, I thought, *they are too young to even know this song, but I'm singing because I don't want the assistant to say anything to the little boy and remind him every five minutes that he has problems.*

So, I began to sing:

He's got the whole world in His hands
He's got the whole wide world in His hands
He's got the whole world in His hands
He's got the whole world in His hands

He's got this *little yellow school bus* in His hands
He's got this *little yellow school bus* in His hands
He's got this *little yellow school bus* in His hands
He's got the whole world in His hands

To my surprise, all the kids knew the song, and we had a little "short bus" choir. When we pulled into the parking lot of the school, all the little handicapped kiddos were singing, "He's got the whole world in His hands." They were smiling, and they were happy.

I pulled up to the place they were to unload, and they were all met by a teacher's aide to escort them into the schoolhouse. I brought the stop light arm in, turned the warning lights off, and began to pull away when the assistant slapped a knee and gushed, "Well, I declare that's the first time *Josh has made it all the way to school since school started"!

I thought to myself, *"You don't get it."*

The only way that we are going to make it to our destination and the only way we can arrive at the place where God wants us is if we all get on the bus *together* – without tearing each other down. Stop and think about passengers riding any bus. The bus has people from all walks of life, different races and backgrounds. We can't sit around and point out each other's problems and faults or we'll have to turn around and begin all over again. The vicious cycle will continue with none of us ever getting to where we need to be.

I've observed this in our churches, businesses and other entities. It seems to become a cycle where the church, organization or business is gaining momentum and picking up speed. It is obvious to everyone that we are on the brink of a breakthrough. Excitement permeates the atmosphere, when out of nowhere someone comes along and begins to finger-point, assign blame, sow discord and we all have to turn around and go back to where we started. This must stop!

We've all got our share of problems; we're all on the short bus of life. We all have fallen short of the glory of God. All I'm asking is for us to get in the same bus! Let us get in one mind and one accord! Let us walk by the same rule! Let us mind the same thing! Let us bind together! Let us lift up holy hands without wrath and doubting! Let us run this race that is set before us! If we have a move of God in our lives, our church, and our districts, it's because we all got onboard and started moving in the same direction. It's up to us because God is willing and wanting us to worship Him, wanting us to push for unity, and wanting us to have revival.

After all, ***"If God be for us, who can be against us!"***[1]

Perhaps you have family members, friends, associates at work that can relate to this story. I believe right now a parent, a schoolteacher or a community leader is receiving inspiration and gaining a deeper understanding of the many benefits of setting a positive example for treating everyone with civility and respect.

Growing a healthy family, church, school, workplace and community is a lifelong process – one that requires constant nurturing and persistence. Everyone has a role to play in building a healthier, more vibrant community. The choices we make at home, work, school, play and worship determine most what creates personal health and community vitality. To a great extent, it's about how we create the settings in our communities that help bring positive change.

---

[1] *Names have been changed to protect the privacy of individuals and their families.

Healthy communities call for inspired leadership and action from every corner of our communities. Today, there's often a gulf between the conversation people have around the kitchen table and the conversations we have with our leaders. We see turf battles and fragmentation of efforts with more resources getting spent on the symptoms of deeper problems and less on what generates health in the first place.

Be encouraged friend! Who else would enjoy hearing this story today?

Chapter Seven

The Godly Influence of My Mother

"And Isaac intreated the LORD for his wife, because she was barren: and the Lord was intreated of him, and Rebekah his wife conceived… And she said, if it be so, why am I thus? And she went to inquire of the LORD."

Genesis 25:21-22

Medical professionals recommend prenatal care, or special health measures for expectant mothers, to enhance the development of an unborn baby. Studies have affirmed the importance of prenatal care to help keep the mother and her baby healthy. Babies of mothers who do <u>not</u> receive prenatal care are three times more likely to have a low birth weight and five times more likely to die than those born to mothers who <u>do</u> receive care.

However, it is just as important for both parents to pray prenatal *prayers* over their unborn child. Children are a sacred trust. They are more than tax deductions; they are meant to be an investment, and pregnancy is an amazing time of impartation to an unborn baby.

I recall my mother telling me many times as a boy, and even reminding me as an adult, "Son, I dedicated you to the Lord before you were even born." As a young mother, even before sonograms, she would place her hand over her abdomen and pray, "God, bless my son, and keep Your hand on him. And, God, if You see fit, You can call him into the ministry and use him for Your work." This kind of praying took place throughout her pregnancy. She would sing songs and pray, then pray and sing more songs. I am her first born and a minister of the Gospel. There is power in prenatal prayer!

The Bible tells us that Hannah prayed before Samuel was ever conceived, and in her prayer she said to God, *"...but wilt give unto thine handmaid a man child, then I will give him unto the LORD all the days of his life"* (I Samuel 1:11). I believe she prayed over Samuel and dedicated him to the Lord during her pregnancy before she ever presented him to Eli. After her prayer, verse eighteen says that Hannah's *"countenance was no more sad."* Both the physical and spiritual condition of the mother is paramount in the overall development of her unborn child, all of which are impacted by prayer.

The story of Jacob's miracle birth underscores the need for prayer as well. It begins with a desire for children and extends to personhood within the womb. Jacob was no "Wednesday's child"; he was a wanted child. Genesis 25:21 reads, *"And Isaac intreated the LORD for his wife, because she was barren: and the LORD was intreated of him, and Rebekah his wife conceived."*

Isaac and Rebekah had been married nineteen years and had no children. James says, *"The effectual prayer of a righteous man availeth much."* Isaac understood this power of prayer and intreated the Lord. The Lord opened the womb of Rebekah, and she conceived! It is interesting to note that later during her pregnancy, Rebekah was concerned about her condition, as well as the condition of her baby. She had no doctor, no sonogram and no professional opinion available. So, she took the matter directly to the Lord. Here is an example of mom and dad offering prenatal prayer. There is power in prenatal prayer!

An important aspect of prenatal prayer is the involvement of family. Paul wrote to his son in the Gospel in II Timothy 1:5 (NIV), *"I have been reminded of your sincere faith, which first lived in your grandmother Lois and in your mother Eunice, and, I am persuaded, now lives in you also."* Timothy did not just wake up one morning after reaching adulthood and decided he wanted to be involved in the work of the Lord. There is evidence in this scripture that his grandmother Lois prayed for her daughter, Eunice. Then Eunice prayed for her son, Timothy, and that same sincere faith was transmitted from one to the other.

In Philippians 2:20, the Apostle Paul proclaimed that there was no one like Timothy, and again in Acts 16:2, he stated that the brothers of Lystra and Iconium spoke well of him (Timothy).

What was it that caused Paul and Luke to make such a *commendable* statement regarding his "son in the faith"? The answer is found in II Timothy 1:5 as Paul recalled the *profound influences* that Timothy had in his life.

Chuck Swindoll says, "If you were blessed with a good mother, you will reap the benefits the rest of your days. If your mother neglected your needs and failed to support your dad, unfortunately, much of what you suffered cannot be erased. For good or ill, a mother's mark is permanent."

And I might add, that mark begins before birth.

Much has been said about prenatal prayer. However, my mother's prayers and influence continued throughout my infancy, childhood, and adolescence. Even up to this very moment, my mother's prayers cover me on a daily basis.

She made sure that her children went to youth rallies, attended youth camp and taught us to be committed to our church. She involved us in Sunday School singing and Bible Drills. I vividly remember her telling us as we were getting dressed for church, "we are going to the House of God, so we will wear our best and go worship our King!" She never permitted her children to go to church slouchy in attire or

53

attitude. She was always excited and enthused about going to church, and her enthusiasm was contagious, and her worship was lively. There was never any question about going to church. It was something we all anticipated.

My mother made up her mind as a young mother with four small children that she was going to raise her children in church and make a difference in their lives. I was present and an eyewitness the night of December 27, 1962 when she received the gift of the Holy Spirit. Because of her prayers and influence, my sweet mother has children, grandchildren and now great-grandchildren full of the Spirit, loving God and involved in church. If the Apostle Paul were writing to me like he did to Timothy, he could possibly write something similar to me as he did to Timothy. "I have been reminded of your sincere faith, which first lived in your mother Faye and your grandmother Lola and, I am persuaded, now lives in you also."

To every mother, father, and Sunday School teacher, you are having a greater influence than you could ever imagine. Keep teaching, praying, and believing. You will reap if you faint not.

I am eternally grateful for my mother, Alice Faye Tipton.

The U.S.S. Astoria was a heavy cruiser, which saw duty during World War II's Battle of the Coral Sea and at Midway, then was sunk in August of 1942 at the Battle of Savo Island. On board in the fight for Savo was Signalman third class Elgin Staples. Sometime around 2 am on the ship's final day, Staples was blown overboard when one of Astoria's gun turrets exploded. In the water, wounded in both legs by shrapnel and in a state of near-shock, Staples was kept afloat by a narrow lifebelt, which he had activated by a trigger.

In his book *The Grand Weaver*, Ravi Zacharias tells the fascinating story of what happened next.

"Four hours after being blown into the Pacific, Staples was picked up by a passing destroyer and returned to the Astoria. Even though the cruiser had been severely damaged, her captain was trying to beach the ship in order to save her. When his attempts failed, Staples found himself back in the water. By now, it was noon.

This time it was the U.S.S. President Jackson that plucked him out of the water. On board, Staples studied the little lifebelt that had saved his life twice that day. He noticed the belt was manufactured by the Firestone Tire and Rubber Company of Akron, Ohio, and carried a registration number.

Allowed to go home for a visit, Staples related his story to the family and asked his mother, who worked for Firestone, the purpose of the registration number on the belt. She pointed out that the company was holding employees responsible for their work in the war effort, and each worker had his/ her own number for quality control. Staples recalled everything about that lifebelt, including the registration number. As he called it out, his mother's eyes grew large. She said, 'That was my personal code that I put on every item I was responsible for approving!'"

His mother had made the belt which had saved his life twice.

Zacharias concludes, "The one who gave birth and whose DNA he bore gave him rescue in the swirling waters that threatened to take his life. If an earthly parent playing the role of procreation can provide a means of rescue without knowing when and for whom that belt would come into play, how much more can the God of all creation accomplish?"

Special thanks to my mother, Alice Faye Tipton, for all her prayers.

A Tribute to My Mother
Alice Faye Tipton

My memories of childhood include the many things my mother did to make sure my dad, siblings and I were well cared for and happy. With five large appetites and a limited budget, my mother and her ability to prepare tasty food could put a spread on the table fit for a king. But my mother did far more than cook for us to let us know she loved us.

These are just a few things that mom did without even one complaint. She kept our clothes clean, hair combed, tended to our scrapes and cuts, drove us to youth rallies, cheered us on at our field day at school, helped us learn how to have fun in a Bible Drill, assisted with our homework, knelt beside our beds to pray, and yes, wiped tears and kissed the pain away, all the while making sure not a child was overlooked, doing or giving whatever each needed, as though she had nothing more important to do. My mother did many other things for me that if I listed one at a time may seem inconsequential, but when woven together, made me who I am.

I am mom's first and best-looking (mom has made each of my siblings to think the same way) son and over the sixty-three years since my birth, I have seen my mother change as she gracefully grew older, but more importantly, I have seen much remain the same through her steadfastness.

She had me when she was seventeen. I often tell people that I helped raise her. Although now much older than the beautiful dark complexion and long flowing hair of a teen mom, she remains a beautiful lady both inside and out. Her eyes still sparkle and offer reassurance to whoever she gazes upon. Her soft touch and continuous smile still warms, as does her laughter and heartfelt embrace that comes from a heart of love.

Thankfully, my mother does not look or act like she is now in her 80's. However, she realizes that as she 'ripens,' her health will require more and more concessions from her. (That's happening to me, too.) Yet, in spite of these natural changes, she always manages to be there when needed.

Mother was born October 24, 1939, the third child of Mayo and Lola Chason. Her dad named her after a famous actress and singer (Alice Jean Leppert) whose stage name was Alice Faye. In 1939, Faye was named one of the top ten box office draws in Hollywood. It was so ironic that mother's dad died on December 19, 1942 when she was only three years old. Not long after his death, the song "You'll Never Know" was introduced in the 1943 movie *Hello, Frisco, Hello* where it was sung by Alice Faye. The song won the 1943 Award for the Best Original Song.

I've always sensed a hole in my mother's heart due to never knowing her dad and missing out on having his hugs and kisses and living with the feeling of, *I will never know.*

I do not know what my mother's dreams were, what plans she had in mind for herself as she grew up, where she wanted to visit or what she might have become if things had been different. But the hardships and enduring testimony of a faithful God were some of the ingredients that made my "Alice Faye" the wonderful person she is. Sure, there are many things I do not know, but there are some things I do know. I know my mother loves God with all of her heart. I do know that she enjoys being a mother, a grandmother, and a surrogate mother or grandmother to those in need who have been fortunate enough to enter her life.

I love my mother dearly, and there are many things I want to do for her, and a few places to go, but most of all, I want to tell her "thank you." I can never repay her for all the things she's given or taught me or express enough gratitude for what she has done. But I know what I will do. I will do what my mother did for me. I will be there when she needs me, no matter what. I love you, Mom.

Your Son,

David D. Tipton, Jr.
December 19, 2014

518 4th Street – Port St. Joe, Florida

Be encouraged friend! Who else would enjoy hearing this story today?

Chapter Eight

No Greater Joy

A Tribute to my Children

"I have no greater joy than to hear my children walk in the truth."

III John 1:4

Dear Devonn,

It's another Father's Day. I suppose a dad cannot help thinking about his children with special concentration on a day such as this. And my thoughts are very strong with you. Oh yes, Damon is very much on my mind, as are those two who joined our family later, Rachael and Matthew.

In lieu of a traditional Father's Day card, I have chosen to write you a "letter of love." Your brother Damon will also receive a similar letter to yours.

I want you to know that I never asked you to be an extension of my life. By that I mean, I would have been just as proud of you had you become a butcher or baker or candlestick maker. But the fact that God called you into His ministry as a worship leader and musician causes me to be very thankful. It is the highest calling of life to be used for God and used for His Kingdom. And the God who called you is more than faithful to see you through every problem and stress you will encounter.

I remember so well the day I was raking yards in Georgetown, Louisiana, and you slipped up behind me holding a thrift store briefcase and told me, "Dad, I am going to be your assistant pastor." You really don't know how much you have assisted me through the years. Your musical abilities, your proofreading and writing skills have made me look smarter than I really am. You are truly a blessing!

You have come a long, long way, Son. During your 33 years on Planet Earth, you have brought many smiles to your folks – and some consternation, too, to be perfectly frank about it. ☺ Regrettably, due to my stubbornness, I was difficult at times and perhaps too hard on you. We probably share that trait. ☺

And the memory is still warm and marvelous as you proposed to your fiancée, Julie on the very top of the Empire State Building in New York City. I was so thankful to God that He brought such a precious young lady into your life. And now God has blessed you both with three beautiful children; Cooper, Anna Kate and Ava Klaire, who bring lots of sunshine to my life.

You have a great mother, Devonn. She nurtured you with love and a firm hand and helped mold you into the man she knew you could be.

Well, son, we never had a very fancy home; I mean, no one ever got our home and the Taj Mahal confused. Our cars were not too sporty or expensive. But we had the Lord. And we talked to Him and about Him and leaned upon His help rather than our own understanding. So, you grew up seeing God work out all things for His glory and pleasure.

In your teen years, you devoted yourself to help your parents in growing a church in Grenada and committed to become the church worship leader. All the hours you spent rehearsing, learning new music and teaching yourself (with God's help) how to play a keyboard has not gone unnoticed. I will always cherish the memory of the first solo you sang in church entitled, "I Know the Master of the Wind."

You know something else you had, Devonn? You had the privilege of growing into manhood in those impressionable years as part of a fantastic church. You helped dad grow a church in Grenada.

We all learned together that we could trust God, didn't we? There were some years our income was quite pathetic. But we had a sacred trust to keep as stewards in the Lord's service. We always tithed and gave sacrificially in offerings.

And I know that you are continuing that practice. That's great Son, for God cannot bless a person who robs Him of His tithes and offerings. Oh, Devonn, God is faithful!

Devonn, I am no expert on raising children. As a result, I know I made a lot of mistakes. Sometimes it's hard to understand our children. But we made it through. And my goodness, look how you turned out! Love is a great teacher and welder of human spirits.

I have had many blessings in my 56 years. But of them all, a happy home is the very best. And from that home have come four children. I could not possibly ask for more than I have had. I thank God for you, Devonn, your brother, Damon and later Rachael and Matthew and your precious mother.

I pray for you a life that is blessed of God in every respect. May those good things that came to you as a child remain with you forever. And may the unfortunate things – those things that you would have changed if you could – be lasting lessons for you as you raise your children and lead your family as priest of your home.

Yes, I've liked the ties and the cards throughout the years. Thanks. But most of all, thanks for being a terrific son. Today, you are ministering the Gospel of our Lord Jesus Christ in song and music. I could not possibly have asked for more. I love you.

Happy Father's Day!

Your Dad
June 16, 2013

Be encouraged friend! Who else would enjoy hearing this story today?

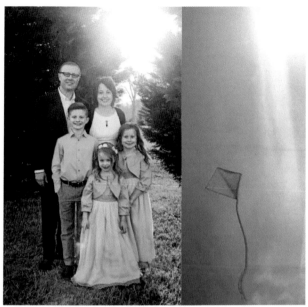

After thirteen years in our family, our precious Julie took flight to her heavenly home on April 16, 2018. She exists now, only in memory; it will be up to others to share the little things that made her who she was. Throughout her journey with cancer, she never gave up in despair and was quick to point out the importance of trusting and leaning on God's everlasting arms to their children and others around her.

God's blessings: On June 27, 2020, we welcomed Leah and her two children into our family. We are so very thankful for her love to Devonn and their new family.

Dear Damon,

It's another Father's Day. I suppose a dad cannot help thinking about his children with special concentration on a day such as this. And my thoughts are very strong with you. Oh yes, Devonn, our firstborn is very much on my mind, as are those two that joined our family, Rachael and Matthew.

In lieu of a traditional Father's Day card, I have chosen to write you a "letter of love." Your brother, Devonn will also receive a similar letter to yours.

I want you to know that I have never asked you to be an extension of my life. By that I mean I would have been just as proud of you had you become a butcher or baker or candlestick maker. But the fact that God called you into His ministry causes me to be very thankful. It is the highest calling of life to be a voice for God. And the God who called you is more than faithful to see you through every problem and stress you will encounter.

I remember so well the night you and I traveled from Corinth. You opened the dialogue about feeling your call to preach. I told you, from this moment on we are fellow ministers, and your ministry, your ideas, reaches more souls, and strengthens more families in commitment to God than my life ever did. And I am confident in my spirit that you will do just that.

You have come a long way, Son. During your 31 years on Planet Earth, you have brought many smiles to your folks – and some consternation to be perfectly frank about it. ☺

I still shake a little when I remember you getting lost in the mall, as your mom and I were panicking trying to find you. I recall as a toddler; you were about to run into a busy street with me chasing you as you thought we were playing chase. I managed to scoop you up just before you stepped off the curb. Whew!

And the memory is still warm and marvelous as you proposed to your fiancée, Kandi on the red bridge at the Botanical Gardens in Memphis. I was so thankful to God that He brought such a precious young lady into your life. And now God has blessed you with three beautiful children; Kanon, Kade, and Darlynn Grace who bring lots of sunshine to my life.

You have a great mother, Damon. She nurtured you with love and a firm hand and helped mold you into the man she knew you could be.

Well, Son, we never had a very fancy home; I mean, no one ever got our home and the Taj Mahal confused. Our cars were not too sporty or expensive. But we had the Lord. And we talked to Him and about Him and leaned upon His help rather than our own understanding. So, you grew up seeing God work out all things for His glory and pleasure.

In your teen years, you gave up being a drummer for the jazz band in the Grenada High School and opted to use those talents for the worship of God.

You know something else you had, Damon? You had the privilege of growing into manhood in those impressionable years as part of a fantastic church. You helped dad grow a church in Grenada.

We all learned together that we could trust God, didn't we? There were some years when our income was quite pathetic. But we had a sacred trust to keep as stewards in the Lord's service. We always tithed and gave sacrificially in offerings.

And I know that you are continuing that practice. That's great Son, for God cannot bless a person who robs Him of His tithes and offerings. And we supported missions as God led us, and now you and I are involved in missions work. I watched you give an extremely poor pastor in the Dominican Republic your nice watch because the Lord impressed you to. I've never seen a broader smile then when that pastor was told that our church would purchase the lot for his church. Oh, Damon, God is faithful!

Damon, I am no expert on raising children. As a result, I know I made a lot of mistakes. Sometimes, it's hard to understand our children. But we made it through. And, my goodness, look how you turned out! Love is a great teacher and welder of human spirits.

I have had many blessings in my 56 years. But of them all, a happy home is the very best. And from that home have come four children. I could not possibly ask for more than I have had. I thank God for you, Damon, your brother Devonn and later Rachael and Matthew and your precious mother.

I pray for you a life that is blessed of God in every respect. May those good things that came to you as a child remain with you forever. And may the unfortunate things – those things that you would have changed if you could – be lasting lessons for you as you raise your children and lead your family as priest of your home.

Yes, I've liked the ties and the cards throughout the years. Thanks. But most of all, thanks for being a terrific son. Today, you are ministering the Gospel of our Lord Jesus Christ. I could not possibly have asked for more. I love you!

Happy Father's Day!

Love, Dad
June 16, 2013

Dear Rachael and Matthew,

Perhaps you've heard someone say or may have said it yourself, "You're not my real mom/ dad" or "he's not my real brother/sister."

In the book Velveteen Rabbit, the rabbit asks the Skin Horse who had lived longer in the nursery than any of the others, "What is real?" I am certain many times in your childhood, you too asked the same question.

Life often throws us curves, and things happen that we don't understand. But I know God allowed you into our home and more importantly, into our hearts. Not having the same last name, or being related biologically, doesn't mean we are not family. You are our family. I remember Matthew telling Devonn and Damon (his big brothers) one day, "Mom and Dad didn't have a choice when you were born, they had to take what they got, but they wanted me."

It is true! We wanted you. We wanted you both to have a home. We wanted you to be loved. We wanted you to feel secure. We wanted the best for your lives.

Rachael, you have blessed us with five beautiful and handsome grandchildren: McKayla, Kamdon, Brantley, Presley and Ellie. Stan is a wonderful husband and provider for his family. We are so proud of you.

Matthew, you for the most part of your life, have been with us. Mom and I enjoyed surprising you with Christmas gifts just to see the joy on your face.

You have never given us any trouble, and you've never had to wonder if someone loves you.

Family isn't whose blood you carry. It's who you love and who loves you back, and you don't have to have the same blood to be family.

Dave Willis said it best, "Family isn't defined only by last names or by blood; it's defined by commitment and love. It means being there when they need it most. It means having each other's backs. It means choosing to love each other even on those days when you struggle to like each other. It means never giving up on each other!

Love, Mom and Dad

Be encouraged friend! Who would enjoy hearing this story today?

Chapter Nine

Stuck in the Mud

"Who having such a charge, thrust them into the inner prison, and made their feet fast in the stocks."

Acts 16:24

It was a cold December day in 1983 as he walked along the mud flats, dipping for trout and other fish that were frozen in the cold water and left stranded when the tide went out. After gathering a sufficient number of fish, he decided to make his way back.

He was a little over 400 yards from the bridge when he began to sink in the mud. He tried to fight. The more he tried to get free, the deeper he would sink. Like quicksand, the mud pulled him down. After sinking in mud up to his waist, he decided to stop fighting. Instinctively, he began to cry out for help.

It wouldn't be too long before the tide came in again. He would either drown or freeze to death. Law enforcement informed him that they had sent a Coast Guard helicopter with a ladder rope and an airboat was trying to be located.

He grew desperate… crying out and praying that God would send someone to help. Authorities spent an hour trying to encourage the man to hold on – help was coming; however, time was running out.

Thankfully, God sent an angel in the form of a man by the name of Sammy Oats. Sammy risked his safety to come to his aid. I am alive today because of his sacrifice.

How many times in our walk with God, do we find ourselves stuck in the mud of life? I am reminded of the words to the old song: *"I was going down for the last time and no one heard my cry. My voice was swiftly fading, drifting with the tide. Then a hand from out of nowhere, gently slipped in mine. And I thank God, He found me... Just in time."*

Heroics bring medal of bravery

A real hero

The reality is that sooner or later, all of us will feel stuck and unable to move. There will always be something trying to hold us down or pull us under. The powers that try to pull us down and away from God can be terrifying when we are left feeling the pain of our own inadequacies. It is natural to panic and hopelessly feel like there is no way that we can make it.

As time passed by – with me stuck in the mud, it was in this moment that God began to speak to me. I do not think that He was the one who caused me to get into this position; however, I believe that He used this opportunity to speak to me in that still, small voice. I remember hearing the Lord tell me that I needed to put my trust in Him more and to rely on His provision.

I had been struggling with the fact that I didn't feel good enough to answer His call. I remember feeling so frustrated... wondering if God had really called me.

So, here I was, stuck in the mud, crying out for my very life; realizing that I needed to be more dependent upon the God who had everything under control. He heard my cry even when I wasn't sure anyone else could… Even when I wasn't sure I was going to make it out of that impossible situation.

Thank God that His ear is not heavy that He cannot hear, and His arm is not short that it cannot reach. When we call out to Him in our despair, He is ready and waiting to rescue. We just have to stop fighting and surrender to His helping hand.

I am reminded of when I was in my early teens. I had felt the call to preach from the age of nine. However, I was very insecure and introverted. I felt so inadequate. How could God use someone that was afraid to speak out? How could I be of service to Him, if I didn't have the talent that others my age did?

I felt so overwhelmed by the sense of being incapable and inadequate. But I could not get past the feeling that God had called me. I would spend my alone time visualizing what it would be like to actually live out my calling.

I would go to car lots and look at full size cars, imagining that I was an evangelist. I would look into the back seat, and I could clearly see my suitcase and briefcase sitting on the back seat along with my Bible and notes. I didn't realize it at the time, but God was keeping the fire of desire for ministry burning in my heart.

On Sundays after lunch, in between services, I would have my mom drop me off at the church alone. I would practice

preaching to an empty building and sit at the piano, playing the only song that I knew how to play. I would nod to my imaginary congregation and begin… *"I can read – I can write – I can smoke my papa's pipe."*

David D. Tipton, Jr. - 1968

Many times, I had to fight back insecurities, rather than dealing openly with my calling. I buried all of my feelings, keeping them hidden from everyone.

Maybe this story resonates with you. Maybe you can identify with the feelings of inadequacy or loneliness and have found yourself questioning if God really called you. I'm telling you now... Keep that fire of desire burning. Even when you feel like you can't make it on your own... I want you to know that... You can succeed! You can live an overcoming life; despite the vacuum of the world trying to pull you down into cold and painful misery. There is nothing in this world more powerful than the testimony of an overcomer. **They make the angels feel insignificant!**

Paul and Silas did not get under their circumstances; they got over their circumstances. They made the chamber of torture a chapel of triumph. They sang and worshipped God despite their situation.

Learn to use your situation as a stimulus and inspiration. No one can fetter your spirit; you're the only one who can do that. Over the years, I have found the rough and painful places of life gave me determination. Some of the best incentive I have had was when people unjustly criticized me or laughed at me. I know that one day I am going to meet some of those jesters at the end of the road and thank them for providing me with opportunities to overcome them. I might not have been able to grow if they had not laughed at me.

You can turn your circumstances around to the glory of God! Make the sick room radiant. Change the ungodly atmosphere where you go to school. Set an example of faithfulness in your home. God will honor your faith! Years ago, a young man came to me after service and said, "Our youth group is falling apart, and God spoke to me and said you're the one to bring it back." God has chosen the weak things of the world to confound the mighty. Remember, it was the little atom when it was loose that won the war. Something within your reach is waiting to be released to produce something great in your life.

Let that be your attitude today. God has a plan for you. He will not leave you where you are… He will come to you. He will provide a way of escape… even in the most difficult of situations. Even when it seems that there is no way… God will make a way. He will send someone to provide you with the encouragement you need to make it through. If God has called you, no one can take it away.

If God is for you… No one can be against you. So, if you feel stuck in the mud, help is on the way!

Jesus is coming to your rescue. Just hold on. Tell yourself continually: I won't look at my difficulty. I will look at every situation as an opportunity. I won't panic, but I will sing even when I'm stuck in the mud. Knowing that my deliverer is on the way!

I was going down for the last time and no one heard my cry. My voice was swiftly fading, drifting with the tide. Then a hand from out of nowhere gently slipped in mine. And I thank God He found me… just in time.

Be encouraged friend! Who else would enjoy hearing this story today?

Chapter Ten

Childhood Memories

I've been born twice. One I cannot remember, the other I'll never forget. The one that I don't remember took place in Gulf Pines Hospital in Port St. Joe, Florida where my seventeen-year-old mother gave birth to me, on January 17, 1957. I am sure my mother remembers this day when her first born due in March arrived a little early (I'd rather be an hour early than one minute late) and weighed in at five pounds and six ounces.

Gulf Pines Hospital – Port St. Joe, Florida

I grew up in the quaint little paper mill town watching the smokestack at St. Joe Paper Company to tell which way the wind was blowing. Dad taught us that when smoke was going straight up that it was a good night to get the gig and go floundering. Dad did not like anyone criticizing the smell of the paper mill. He would always say, "that smells like bacon and eggs to me," meaning this is where he earned his living to provide us with food and shelter.

In these formative years I learned about life, family, neighbors, and developed a work ethic that still follows me to this day. At nine years old, I put in to get a job. I was so persistent about going to work that my dad finally agreed to take me to Jack Hammock's Barbershop to see if he would let me shine shoes. Mr. Hammock told me that if I would keep the shop clean, I could shine shoes in his barbershop. At fifty cents a pair, I would shine shoes and sweep floors.

After I had a little money in my pocket, I would hop on my bicycle, ride up Reid Avenue to First Street, turn left one block, and on the corner was Mr. Aubrey Tomlinson's Gulf Station. I would put a dime in the drink machine and pull out a refreshing Pepsi and give him a nickel for a Hershey's Bar and sit there with Mr. Tomlinson while I took "my break." This is where I became addicted to Pepsi and Hershey's candy bars. On other occasions, I would go across the street from the barbershop to Smith's Pharmacy and sit on one of the many stools in front of the bar at the soda fountain and Betty Brooks Clift would make me a cherry coke.

I felt like an adult the day I walked into Roach's Furniture Store and said to Mrs. Roach that I would like to buy something for my mother for Mother's Day. She allowed me to put a flowerpot that sat in a wrought iron stand on layaway. I paid a little every week until I paid it in full.

Since I was a working "man," I also committed to a pledge of fifty cents a week to support our campground in Ocala, Florida. I am still seeking support for our district campground in Mississippi. I started early.

Reid Avenue – Port St. Joe, Florida

My dad got paid on Thursdays, and I could set my watch to when my mother and siblings would take my dad's check to Rich's IGA to cash the check and buy groceries. I would leave the barbershop a couple blocks away and ride my bike to the store. Sure enough, our vehicle would be in the parking lot. I would go into the store and head for the meat counter and pick out a pack of pork chops that had six chops in it. Then I would lift it from the meat counter and find my mother in the store and take money from my wallet, hand it to mom and say, "Mom, I'd like to have pork chops this week."

My mother could buy one chicken and find so many ways to cook and use it during the week. I don't think we ever knew she was being creative with her culinary skills.

I was shining this man's shoes one day and he said to me, "How would you like to learn a trade?" To which I replied, "How much will it cost me?" That's a huge question for a ten-year-old. He made a statement I had never heard before. He

said, "It will not cost you anything, you earn while you learn."
I said, "What do you do?" He said, "I own an upholstery shop,
and I'd like for you to go to work with me." He had already
spoken with my dad, so I made arrangements with Mr.
Hammock and gave him my "notice." With the huge salary of
$1.00 per day, I was now an employee of Mr. Johnny Walker
at Johnnie's Trim Shop.

Johnnie's Trim Shop

I did not realize what Mr. Walker was doing until it
dawned on me one day after I was grown. He gave me a
twenty-dollar bill and said, "Hop on your bike and run over
to IGA and get me a bar of Lava soap." Twenty dollars in
1967 was a lot of money to a boy making a dollar a day! I did
as I was told and remember vividly asking the cashier for the
receipt. When I returned to the upholstery shop, I handed him
the bar of soap, the receipt, and his change. I didn't realize he
was checking my honesty.

Mr. Walker was a shift worker at the paper mill and in the
summer, he would allow me to open the shop, answer the
phone, take messages and write receipts to customers who
had stopped by to pay on their bill. He would have me put the
money in a cigar box in his desk drawer.

Mr. Walker added a bicycle repair shop inside the upholstery shop and put me on commission. Along with Curtis Little, I would repair bicycles and sell parts. I worked for Mr. Walker until I was thirteen the summer of 1970. Seems like my last paycheck was nearly $60.00. For a brief period of time, I also sold The Grit newspaper and was a substitute paper delivery boy for The Star.

Another childhood memory I will never forget occurred when I was five years old and my brother, Steve was four.

We found a box of matches and one of us had the idea, (I'll take the blame, I'm the oldest!) to go out in the field and play with those matches.

We went out in the middle of dry sage grass taller than us boys, squatted down and began to take turns striking matches so we could see the spark. We would then toss the match aside and light another. We were not aware the grass around us had caught on fire.

Mrs. Wise, our neighbor, saw us and the fire and began to scream out, "Faye! The field is on fire, and your boys are in the field!"

My mother ran out the back door, jumped off the porch and like a deer ran into the field, jumping flames and through the fire.

She got to us and grabbed us up – one boy on each hip. She jumped and ran back through the fire. When she got us to safety, she began to hug us and say, "Mother could've lost you boys! I love you so much!" And then she bent us over her knee and tore us up and said, "Don't you ever play with matches again, you hear me?!" Then she turned us around and hugged us again. She alternated between these two processes a few times.

Her method of parenting was effective *and* scriptural. *"Foolishness is bound in the heart of a child; but the rod of correction shall drive it far from him,"* **Proverbs 22:15.**

Be encouraged friend! Who else would enjoy hearing this story today?

Chapter Eleven

Do You See It?

"Now faith is the substance of things hoped for, the evidence of things not seen."

Hebrews 11:1

As I continue to reflect on many of my childhood memories, my mind has taken me back to Port St. Joe Elementary School where I attended from first to sixth grade. I was extremely blessed to have been taught by some of the very best teachers a child could have. I pay tribute to each of my elementary school teachers.

First Grade:	Charlotte Nedley
Second Grade:	Betty Sue Anchors
Third Grade:	Willie Mae Daniels
Fourth Grade:	Angela Stone
Fifth Grade:	Betty Sue Anchors
Sixth Grade:	Frank Barnes

Each of these, in their own unique style, instilled principles in me and made learning fun. The influence of a good teacher can never be erased. The power of their presence in the lives of others can leave a remarkable imprint.

Once, in the Bureau of Standards in Washington, D.C., a tiny tube containing less than 1/2,000 of an ounce of radium was accidentally dropped and broken on the hardwood floor. With a camel's hairbrush, they swept up the radium. Then they washed the floor to get the rest of it. But enough remained to render four more washings necessary. Each yielded more radium. Finally, a carpenter scraped the floor three years later, the shavings were burned, and the ashes were found to be strong in radium. INFLUENCE! Teachers influence the world.

I will never forget Mrs. Nedley bringing in the black and white TV into our classroom and letting us watch with shock and sadness, the live coverage of the assassination of President John F. Kennedy. This was my first introduction, in my memory, to life in the real world where I had to meet triumph and disaster and as Rudyard Kipling put it, treat those two imposters just the same. My teacher was exposing her class to a lesson – preparing us for adulthood and our journey into the future. We still recited the Pledge of Allegiance to the Flag, and prayer was offered over the Public Address system then.

Even though Mrs. Nedley made me feel like I was her favorite (I'm sure all her students felt the same), it did not keep her from administering proper discipline.

I'm not sure why I did it. But as I recall, we were in the lunchroom, and I was sitting next to my friend, Jeremiah Perna. All of a sudden, I filled up my spoon with rice from off of my plate and quickly dumped it down the back of

Miss Lovelace/Nedley
1st Grade
1963-64

Jeremiah's collar. What really got me was when Mrs. Nedley told me, "David, I am so disappointed in you." To disappoint her, hurt me more than the punishment of having to stand by the pole all week during recess while my classmates were playing. School is a whole lot more than academics.

Just in case I didn't apologize, I'm sorry Jeremiah!

Recently, my grandsons and I had a wonderful visit with Mrs. Nedley. They thought it was 'really cool' to get to meet my first-grade teacher. Unfortunately, she passed just a few months after. I was so glad for the opportunity to thank her once again.

Mrs. Betty Sue Anchors was the motherly, nurturing teacher who seemed to always know when you needed a hug and could make you feel ten feet tall. She loved every single student she taught.

Fourth grade was unique in many ways. It was the year our school integrated. I remember the first black student in our class. He and I were in Mrs. Stone's (4th Grade) and Mr. Barnes' (6th Grade) class together. His name was Smiley Shackleford. He and I remained friends until we moved three years later.

What I appreciate about Mrs. Stone is that she was a spontaneous person. And she used her spontaneity to teach her students. One morning, she began class by saying "I am going to teach you a lesson by observation today." She said, "I am going to walk around the classroom, and I'd like for you to see if you can find anything about me that is odd or different." She walked up and down each row, back and forth across the front of the class. No one could figure it out.

She finally agreed to tell us. She explained that she was running late for school and in her haste, she reached into her closet and pulled out a pair of shoes and didn't realize until she got to class that she had one black shoe and one brown shoe on her feet. I've made it my purpose in life to be observant, and as Paul said it by telling us to walk circumspectly.

Mrs. Stone
4th Grade Class

My Sixth grade was probably my most difficult year. It definitely was an advantage to have Mr. Frank Barnes as my teacher. Always, on his first day of class, he would demonstrate how a one-armed man could tie his shoe faster than anyone in his class. Periodically, he would put his foot up on a chair and untie his shoe and tie it back without saying a word. He was the kind of man who would not accept excuses. He not only taught, but he also exemplified how a person could do whatever they set their mind to do, regardless of any disadvantages. He did so many amazing science projects that would capture your mind. It was a special time when he would read Tom Sawyer and use different voices for each character.

Mrs. Willie Mae Daniels was stern, but always fair. Even in 1966, I think she would be honored if someone called her old school. She convinced me to sing in the chorale for the elementary Christmas play. I enjoy singing even unto this day.

Mr. Barnes
6th Grade
1968-69

The title of this chapter comes from this story. While sitting in class with our books opened to the subject being studied, all of a sudden (she would do this every so often), Mrs. Stone spoke up and said, "Okay class, put your books away." She continued, "For the next few moments, I am going to teach you how to use your imagination."

She taught me how to take a trip and never leave the farm. I'm not suggesting smoking weed here; I've never done that. But with an encyclopedia and a little imagination, I've taken some great inexpensive vacations around the world. We were sitting in class one block from St. Joseph Bay and she would say, "Now, close your eyes and imagine with me a beautiful body of clear blue water and around this body of water is pure white sand." With enthusiasm she would say, "Do you see it?"

Each student would say, "Yes ma'am, we see it!"

"Keep your eyes closed. Now I am putting tall palm trees around in the white sand around this beautiful body of water. "Do you see it?" she would exclaim. "Let's continue. In the middle of this beautiful body of blue water, pure white sand, and tall waving palm trees is a small rowboat. Is it there?"

"Yes ma'am, Mrs. Stone, WOW!"

"Let's keep going, class. We are going to think outside the box with our creativity. Paint it in your mind, the beautiful body of blue water, surrounded by pure white sand, with palm trees lined up around the shoreline with a rowboat in the middle of the water. Now, I want you to put a pink elephant in the rowboat. Do you see it?"

To our amazement, we were learning to visualize.

As I began to get a little older, still somewhat shy, I would have been embarrassed to admit this to my classmates - on those Saturday mornings that dad would take us to car lots to look at cars - when other boys my age were looking at muscle cars like Plymouth Road Runners, Mach I's, Cutlass 442's – I would look around and make sure no one was watching me, and I would find the largest four-door nerd car on the lot and look inside. In my imagination, there was my Thompson Chain Bible resting on the front seat. In the back seat was a clothes rod, and hanging on that rod were several suits, white shirts, and neckties.

On the floorboard was a briefcase full of red-hot sermons that was going to turn the world upside down (I'm still looking for that briefcase). Even though at this time, I would never think about standing behind a podium and preaching the Word, I would close my eyes and visualize myself preaching.

When a little boy or girl searches for heroes, they most likely will bury themselves in books because heroes are made up of great people in history. The histories of a great athlete like a "Babe Ruth", or a soldier like Ulysses S. Grant; Annie Sullivan, an American teacher, best known for being the teacher and lifelong companion of Helen Keller; Clara Barton, a pioneering American Nurse who later founded the American Red Cross, or a leader in difficult times as Abraham Lincoln.

As a boy, I dreamed of preaching – I've done it. I've dreamed of recording a professional project in a real studio in Nashville – I've done it, twice. I dreamed of writing a book – this will be my third.

In all my dreams, I've heard voices and felt inadequate and controlled by inferior complexes. I would always go back to the scripture, If *God is for me, He will equip me. If I can dream it, with His help, I can do it.*

The things I hoped for became evidence of things I've visualized before they became a reality. DO YOU SEE IT?

Be encouraged friend! Who else would enjoy hearing this story today?

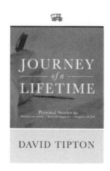

Chapter Twelve

You Got to Move

"And the angel of the Lord spake unto Philip, saying, Arise, and go toward the south unto the way that goeth down from Jerusalem unto Gaza, which is desert."

Acts 8:26

God has been so good to me! Because of jobs, relocations, and pastoral transitions, I have been blessed to have several pastors. Under each of their care and shepherding, I learned many things while being taught the Word of God. In no way do I want to disrespect or say anything disparaging about a minister. My mother taught us children not to touch God's anointed. She put the fear of God in us!

However, preachers are human and are not infallible. In every instance in my life when I did not understand something my pastor or a minister did, God helped me to submit and trust Him with the outcome. Invariably, some of these matters took years to understand, but I have seen God use those very things to ultimately bring me to where I am today.

I have served in many capacities in the local church. At twelve, I was elected to serve as president of our youth class.

I've been a worship leader, youth leader (that's what it was called in those days), Sunday School teacher, and assistant to the pastor. So, I've experienced different leadership styles in and out of the pulpit of the churches I've been blessed to be a part of.

One example: Many years ago, my wife and I were attending a conference when I heard a knock on my hotel door. I opened the door, and an elder was standing there. He said to me, "David, I've been asked to emcee the service today. Will you lead us in worship?"

I said, "Yes sir, I'll be happy to do that."

He said, "Okay. Before you come to church today, you go back in your room and shave your sideburns off."

That stung me! First, I thought to myself, *"You're not my pastor, I don't have to do this!"* However, before I spoke out an inner voice said to me, *"Your spirit is being checked. It's not about your sideburns, it's about your spirit."* In reality, I didn't have sideburns. I'd only been shaving two years and had cut myself both times! It didn't hurt me to do as he asked; however, I led worship that day with a freedom that I would not have **experienced** had I rebelled.

On another occasion, I was so shocked and hurt when my pastor announced from the pulpit that if the tithing didn't pick up, he was going to ask my wife and I to leave. The man next to me said, "Did you know anything about this?"

I said, "No." I don't know if the pastor was trying to see an increase in the tithing or strongly and publicly letting me know it was time for us to go.

About fifteen minutes later, the pastor looked at me and said into the microphone, "Do you know that song, *"You Got to Move*?"

I said, "Yes sir."

He said, "Come lead us in that song."

So, I rushed to the pulpit and while I was hurting inside, I did what the pastor asked me to do and I began to sing:

> You got to move
> You got to move
> You got to move

When the Lord gets ready
You got to move.

You may be high
You may be low
You may be rich
You may be poor
But when the Lord gets ready
You got to move
You got to move.

It's funny now to look back and see how God orchestrated and ordered our steps.

Even in the midst of my confusion and pain; the power of God moved into the sanctuary, and many people were touched by God's Spirit.

Shortly afterward, my little family did move, and we embarked on a journey of trusting God. We found ourselves living in a mobile home that someone kindly allowed us to use at no costs. We were apprehensive about how we were going to make it. So many friends, to name a few: the Mortensen's, Hagan's and the Smith's, were led by God in various ways and several times, when no one knew what we were going through.

I made a personal commitment when I started preaching; I would never call a pastor and invite myself to preach. I am of the opinion that I can be a better blessing to the congregation by being invited by their pastor, than for me to invite myself. Without exception, God never let us down. A number of times it would be late Saturday evening and I would say to my wife, "Well, it looks like we are not going to have a place to preach tomorrow." I remember on a couple of occasions around nine o'clock at night, Pastor Doug Belgard would call me and say, "Brother Tipton, I was down praying and the Lord brought you to mind. You wouldn't happen to be available tomorrow, would you?"

I would say, "Let me look at my schedule and see. Why yes, Brother Belgard, I just happen to have this weekend open." Usually, we would break out into a two-week revival. God is faithful.

One day my wife courageously told me, "Honey, all we have in the pantry today for lunch is a can of white potatoes and I'm not sure we have enough propane (we had a five-gallon propane bottle attached to the stove) for me to even cook the potatoes." She opened the can of potatoes, poured them into a pan, and yes, you guessed it. The bottom of the pan barely got warm when the flame went out. About that time, Crystal Vickery pulled up to the front door and greeted her. She said, "I'm on my lunch break and just stopped by to check on you all."

Well, I was going to be Mr. Hospitality and I said to her, "We are about to have lunch, would you care to join us?" Knowing and hoping she would say, "No, thank you. I have somewhere to go." Can you believe she said, "I believe I will join you all for lunch." When she stepped inside the door, my wife and I began to cry and explain our situation. We had too much "pride" to ask for anything. Remember, you got to move!

That evening my family and I had to go somewhere and when we returned home and entered the door to that mobile home, we saw a living room lined with bags full of groceries. Inside the fridge was milk, round steak (bologna), other kinds of lunch meats, and in the freezer was frozen meat. God knew we had a need and earlier, He had nudged Sister Vickery to check on us. Like David said, "*Once I was young, now I am old, and I've never seen the righteous forsaken or His seed begging for bread.*"

What looks like a bad move is really a God move. These moves led us to pastor our first church, the wonderful congregation in Georgetown, Louisiana. We made the move to Mississippi after being elected in November 1993 to pastor The Pentecostals of Grenada. I firmly believe that I would not be serving as District Superintendent of the Mississippi District had someone not said, "You got to move!"

Be encouraged friend! Who else would enjoy hearing this story today?

Chapter Thirteen

Lucky 13

Written by Gwenda Tipton

"Children's children are a crown to the aged, and parents are the pride of their children."

Proverbs 17:6 NIV

I once read where someone said, "I don't care how poor a man is; if he has a family, he's rich." Rich is an understatement when describing my feelings for my family. God blessed me with wonderful parents who were honest, hardworking, church-going people.

It all began on February 18, 1933 when my parents, Norman Hirkele (Bill) Hayes and Goldie Perdue were united in Holy Matrimony. That same year, while expecting her first child, mother's appendix burst. Due to the severe infection that had set in, she lost her son, Norman Leo. Her physician then informed her that she would be unable to have any more children. Two years later, she proceeded to carry and birth thirteen more children, starting with Norma Jean (died, age 18 months of poliomyelitis), followed by Shelby June, Farrell LaVaughn, Ercel Lucille, Joel Norman, Jeremiah, Paul Thomas (died, age 6 months of pneumonia), Richard Ray, Rebekah Sue, Jacob Lynn, Phillip Darrell, **Gwenda** Joyce (Myself) and Billy Mack. If you're counting, I was child number 13. I know that God told Adam to replenish the earth. However, I think my dad was sure that God was talking to him.

Hayes Family – November 1956

The number thirteen (13) is considered an **unlucky** number in some countries. The end of the Mayan calendar's 13th Baktun was superstitiously feared as a harbinger of the apocalyptic 2012 phenomenon. Fear of the number 13 has specifically recognized phobia, triskaidekaphobia, a word coined in 1911. Some hotels will skip the number 13 on an elevator. The button will go from 12 to 14. However, in Italy, 13 is considered a lucky number. The expression *fare tredici* (to do 13), means to hit the jackpot.

I was born in the Green County Hospital in Paragould, Arkansas on Monday, January 30, 1956, the only child of my parents to be born in a hospital. Dwight D. Eisenhower was our President. An interesting fact that I learned recently is the movie, *Invasion of the Body Snatchers* (I've never seen it), was released that year. Well, that will help me share with you what happened on the day of my birth.

My mother recalled after she delivered me, that a nurse said to her, "Mrs. Hayes, you've given birth to a beautiful, red-headed **girl**."

An hour or so later, a nurse walked back into the room and placed a baby wrapped in a blanket into her arms. It was a little boy! My mother quickly questioned the nurse. "I vaguely remember someone telling me that I had a little red-headed girl." The nurse retrieved the infant boy and said, "Let me go check, Mrs. Hayes."

Sure enough! The nurse returned with a little red-headed girl and placed me into her arms. There's no question that I belonged to the Hayes family – each sibling favoring our parents in one way or another.

Occasionally, my mother and I would be in town, and she would point out to me and say, "There's the boy who was placed in my arms." The nurse had mixed up two different babies and brought her someone else's baby boy!

Fall 1956

Well, I'm not Italian, but I hit the jackpot! I have an amazing Christian Heritage. Our parents instilled a work ethic into each child.

My mother taught me to cook and by example, taught me the principles of holiness and keeping house. She was such an industrious person. Mother was certainly a Proverbs 31 Lady. She left us way too early when she passed in 1978, the year I got married.

My dad was not afraid of hard work. Long before I was born, he along with a team of mules, would cut down the hardwood trees with a crosscut saw and "snake" the logs out of the woods. He would work every day, come home for dinner and shower, then load up the family vehicle and go to church somewhere. My dad never wasted a minute. If he wasn't working or preaching, he would be reading his Bible and studying the Word.

I use the phrase "lucky 13" loosely because of the connotation that 13 is unlucky. I am neither lucky nor unlucky. I AM BLESSED!

My three greatest blessings all came in the month of March. On March 11, 1978, I said, "I DO" to my beloved husband. His good and generous heart shapes everything he does. He's fun and wise, knowing the right thing to say to keep life's craziness in perspective. More than anything, though, he's capable of the deepest, most steady kind of love. The kind that makes our family strong and happy. I am thankful that he stood and like Joshua said, *"As for me and my house, we will serve the Lord."* (Joshua 24:15). We have traveled many miles together. Some roads have been rough, some smooth. Yet I don't regret one single mile.

On March 28, 1980 at 8:19 PM, we were blessed with our firstborn son, David Devonn Tipton, III. Our second blessing Damon Nathaniel Tipton arrived on March 7, 1982 at 1:50 PM. God knew just what we needed, two amazing sons! I could never begin to express what a blessing they have been to us. Their hearts are set on heaven, and this mother has no greater joy than to hear that my children walk in truth (III John 1:4).

The name of this chapter is Lucky Thirteen. This came about as we were sitting in Piccadilly eating lunch with our son, Damon. I was telling the story of my birth and about being the 13th child. I had just finished telling him how my mother had been given the wrong baby. My son exclaimed, "Oh, mom! You've got to tell that story and call it, Lucky Thirteen!" So – here we go!

As a child, my parents instilled faith into my heart very early. I believed, and still do trust God to do anything! I have numerous stories and miracles to tell, but I will share just a few.

We were in a service just a few years ago. The pastor was going around to different people and asking when they had received the Holy Ghost. I immediately started to feel anxious and was very nervous! When I received the Holy Ghost and was baptized, we did not receive certificates. I do remember that I was eight years old, but I don't remember the exact date. I thought to myself, "What am I going to say when he asks me?" All of a sudden, a wonderful feeling full of peace came over me and a still voice said, "You may not remember the day or time, but you can take them to the place." The year was 1964. I was born in 1956, I am now 64, and that was 56 years ago!

I still remember that night and my precious stepmom, Eva Thrasher Hayes, praying with me. I didn't get baptized until I was nine. Brother Cecil and Sister Juanita Evans from Kennett, Missouri came and held a tent revival on our land.

They baptized me in a horse trough. I will never forget that special day!

In the Fall of 1964, our family along with many other families attended a tent revival twenty miles away in Jonesboro, Arkansas. Reverend E.E. Duncan was the minister. We attended the Sunday morning service and wanted to be at the night service, so all the families decided to spend the afternoon at the park and had a picnic while the children played.

There was a tall slide and all of the kids were taking turns, climbing up, sliding down. It was my brother's turn. Jacob turned around and asked Teresa, my best friend (now my Sister-In-Love), if she wanted to go ahead of him. She said no, but I quickly answered, "I will!"

Best Friends –

Teresa Thrasher Hayes and Gwenda Hayes Tipton

I managed to climb past Teresa and sat down. I should have known that my brother was up to something when he offered for someone else to go first. As I went to slide, he quickly sat next to me and tried to go down with me. He was bigger than me, and the slide was very narrow. I tipped over the side and fell to the ground, breaking my arm. I jumped up and ran screaming towards my mom. She was the first to reach me. She straightened my arm out, and I fell straight back to the ground in pain.

They quickly placed me in the front seat of the car, which had a bench seat that went all the way across. Mom placed a pillow under my arm. She and dad began to discuss if they should take me to the Jonesboro or Paragould Hospital. I had never been to the doctor before. I had only been to a Health Clinic to get my immunization shots. I looked at my dad, "Please don't take me to the hospital. Take me to the Preacher and let him pray for me."

That's all it took for my dad to turn the car towards the evangelist quarters where Brother Duncan was staying. As we pulled up, he was coming out of the church. Dad explained what had happened and that I wanted him to pray for me. We got out of the car and Brother Duncan laid hands upon me and prayed a simple prayer. Mom put me back in the car, and they talked for a few minutes, discussing whether we should stay for church or go ahead and head back home to Paragould.

I wanted to stay, so we did. I had my arm resting on a pillow during the service, so mom sat with me in the back row of the tent. In the middle of service, Brother Duncan told the story of what had happened to me. He said I had had a lot of faith, and he wanted to pray for me again.

So, I went to the front. While they prayed, I lifted both arms and trusted that God had already healed me. When we got home, mom wrapped my arm with a piece of cardboard and cloth bandages so that my arm would stay straight. They kept me home over the next couple of days.

I never had another problem with that arm!

A few months later, we had a Sunday dinner at our church. Jacob, who was the culprit behind the slide fiasco – was sitting on the back of a truck. We were playing Tag with all the kids. As he sat there, another kid came by and SWIPE – tagged him. It threw him off balance, and he fell out of the truck. They took him to the hospital and placed his arm in a cast. When our parents took Jacob back for his check-up a few months later, the arm had not healed properly. They needed to re-break and reset his arm. It never was the same.

That is the difference between *a* physician and *THE* Physician!

Another such miracle: I was ten years old and was suffering from a severe asthma attack. My parents sat up all night with me. Morning came, and I was still unwell. I still had never been to the doctor at this point in my life. They decided now was the time. They were taking me to the hospital.

My dad put me in the car, and we began to drive. He suddenly began to speak. He mentioned that the missionary to Mexico was back home. "Do you want me to stop by there and see if he will pray for you?" I agreed.

We knocked on their door. Brother Johnson stepped out onto his porch. They laid hands on me and prayed. As they talked afterwards, I began to play with their children. A few minutes later, we got back in the car and began to head home. Just another work of the gentle hand of the Great Physician.

Goldie Perdue Hayes

Six hundred university students were asked the question: What is the most important word in the English language? Four hundred twenty-two replied, "Mother." Mother is the most beautiful word. Theodore Roosevelt said, "The United States' most precious asset is our Mothers."

You know there is something about motherhood that is closest to divinity. There is just something about what a mother can do for children, society, and for the church that no one else can do.

Thank God, He put me in the arms of my loving mother! As I look back over the 22 years that my mom was in my life,

I'm reminded that she was a lady who fell in love with God many years before I even came along.

My mother taught me many things. Some things I couldn't understand then, but oh! How I understand and appreciate them now. I am thankful for all the hard work she put into molding and building me.

It makes me understand that saying, *"Mother, your children will never love you as much as you love them. But you can teach them to love their children like you loved them."*

One of the first things my mom taught me, was how to pray. She was an example to me and taught me how to be faithful to the house of God. As I grew up, life was not always easy. We went through hard times, and I've seen my mother crying out to the Lord, reading scriptures, believing in God and His miracles. And He brought us through!

My mother taught me to work. No, I didn't understand (at the time), why my friends could play all the time and I had to clean, sweep, and cook. I remember cooking a whole meal by myself when I was in the 5th grade. Sure, there was some play time; however, there was always more work than play. It was work for her to teach me, but she was building who I would become.

My mom was a good cook. She could make something out of nothing. She invented 'making do.' She planted a garden every year. She canned and put food in the freezer for hard times.

She was a good seamstress and made all of my clothes. I have no memories of shopping for clothes before I got my first job at age 16. She either made them or someone gave me their hand-me-downs. I remember her making clothes out of flour sacks. We couldn't afford china or nice dinnerware, so we would collect the glasses that came out of the Duz

Detergent and the oatmeal boxes. The list goes on and on of the many things my mother taught me.

When I first got my driver's license, mom would let me go into town. But, when I got back, the questions began: "Where did you go? Who did you see? Who did you talk to?" I didn't truly understand then, but she was protecting me. She watched what I did, and she cared what I would become.

My mother could not fix my life, but she set before me an example. She instilled in me a mindset and a heart to look beyond myself for wisdom. She taught me to love God and to lean on Him. She demonstrated a faith that made Him real to me.

My mother is not with me today, but I give her honor for the things she instilled in me. They have been a positive influence on who I am today. They are still with me, and her memory lives on. She was a queen without a crown.

Goldie Perdue Hayes

God blessed me with three sisters who are an inspiration to me. Shelby, Lucy, and Becky.

Lucy was like a second mom to me, and for that I will always be grateful.

Becky, I never dreamed that when I went to stay with you at Tyndall Air Force Base in the summer of 1973 and you took me to the Apostolic Pentecostal Church in St. Andrews, Florida that I would meet the love of my life.

It's amazing to think of all of the changes through the years, but it's wonderful to know that through it all – our faith, friendship, and our love for each other has never wavered. I am truly blessed to have been born in a family with such wonderful loving brothers and sisters.

Farrell LaVaughn Hayes

Norman Herkele (Bill) Hayes

Daddy Was An Old Time Preacher Man

Songwriters: Dorothy Owens/ Dolly Parton

Daddy was an old-time preacher man
He preached the word of God throughout the land
He preached so plain a child could understand
Yes, Daddy was an old-time preacher man

He told the people of the need to pray
He talked about God's wrath and judgement day
He preached about the great eternity
He preached hell so hot that you could feel the heat

Yes, Daddy was an old-time preacher man
Aunt Leanona would get up to testify
And we'd sing "In The Sweet By and By"
Then we'd sing "I'm On My Way To Canaan Land"
Yes, Daddy was an old-time preacher man

Revivals and camp meetings went for weeks
Folks came from all around to hear him preach

Daddy said if one is saved, it's worth it all
But the aisles were always filled at altar calls
Yes, Daddy was an old-time preacher man

Daddy worked for God but asked for no pay
For he believed that God provides a way
We never had a lot but we got by
Guess it's 'cause the Lord was on Daddy's side
Yes, Daddy was an old-time preacher man

Some of my fondest childhood memories are of traveling to street meetings with my daddy. We would travel to Arbyrd, Cardwell, Hornersville, Lapanto, Marked Tree, Tyronza as well as into our own hometown of Paragould. He would park on a street corner. With loudspeakers attached to his car, he would have me sing. After I sang, he would hand me a dime, or a quarter, and I would head off to a store while he preached. I was a paid musician and trained to shop!

It's obvious that Adam had no childhood, but I am so very thankful that I had one which included a rich history, and beautiful memories were created.

The Biggest Little Man

*(Based on a poem given to David Tipton to honor
Norman Terhurst and shared at my dad's funeral.)

He was of small stature,
About five feet two.
Let me tell you his real size,
He was the biggest little man that I ever knew.

He walked each day with his temper soft and cool.
Always so mild, gentle preaching and singing too.
One thing I can tell you, which is very true.
He was the biggest little man that I ever knew.

A friend to everyone he met.
A favor he would never forget
So many folks to church he brought,
Their soul's redemption was what he sought.
He stayed by them to pray them through.
He was the biggest little man I ever knew.

When we have crossed the River Jordan,
To that beautiful Golden shore,
Bill Hayes still will be…
The biggest little man you'll ever see

May God Bless the Memory of
My Wonderful Parents!

Norman Hirkele (Bill) Hayes
Born: February 5, 1911
Died: July 20, 1992

Goldie Lela Gertrude Perdue
Born: January 6, 1916
Died: December 14, 1978

Married: February 18, 1933

Be encouraged friend! Who else would enjoy hearing this story today?

Chapter Fourteen

Stay Humble and Don't Quit

I hate it when a call like this comes in. It has happened to me more times than I care to recall. Recently, a pastor shared this scenario with his peers:

A young man the pastor had married years ago died suddenly. The family said he wasn't going to church and didn't have a pastor, but they asked the pastor to preach the funeral since the pastor had performed the wedding ceremony. As their former pastor, he agreed and said to himself, "I'll do my best, for them and for the Lord. But I hate this sort of thing".

I understand exactly what the pastor meant. I hate anyone not going to church, but especially young couples. I hate funerals, but especially funerals for the unprepared people of whom I know so little.

But as much as I hate it, I'll do my best because of the call of God on my life.

I hate it when a church member decides to oppose the pastor just because they have chosen not to like him. I've seen situations like that where the person criticized the pastor for not coming to see her in the hospital as much as she felt he should. She looked him in the eye and said, "You have not done one positive thing for our church." She was wrong of course. Way wrong.

The former pastor could only reply that when he was her minister, he visited her regularly in the hospital and called on her family members numerous times. He married and buried her family, and she still disliked him and opposed him. So, apparently, it didn't really matter whether he visited her or not.

I hate those situations. I hate the way people take out their bad mental health on the one person God sends to bless them, particularly when he is one of the nicest guys you'll ever meet.

No matter how hard you try, you'll never be able to get everything right. You'll forget people's names; forget they were in the hospital. You'll preach too deep for some and too shallow for others. You'll miss their calls, taking other people's calls. Your every move will be scrutinized. Honestly, some people will place expectations on you that they would never be willing to live up to themselves.

People will criticize you for the silliest things... the car you drive, the house you live in, the shoes you wear... you name it. I'm too liberal for some, I'm too conservative for others, etc. It is easier to receive criticism from people who know you and love you than from people who feel called to the ministry of interference. Wounds from a friend can be trusted. By the way, I have zero respect for someone who leaves a church via email or text message. I don't even waste my time responding to such immaturity. If you don't have the decency to look your pastor in the eye, the same pastor who has prayed and fasted for you, spent time shepherding you, counseling you, loving you, etc., then that speaks volumes about where you are in your faith. **JESUS** teaches us better than that. I have had people take a portion of my sermon and twist it completely out of context and then have the nerve to misquote me to the point of sowing discord in the church. There is one thing that I don't want on my resume – that I cause division in my church.

Someone asked a veteran pastor, "What does it take to stay at a church like yours for many years?" He didn't hesitate in replying, "The skin of a rhino."

I hate that. I understand it, I appreciate the truth of it, and I admire him more than I can put into words. But I hate the reality that serving the Lord's people over long years requires calluses and tough skins.

The reality of the situation is that nothing about this is new. On issuing the call of Jeremiah into the ministry, the Lord said, *"You will go to all to whom I send you, and whatever I command, you shall speak."* Then He added, *"Do not be afraid of their faces,"* **(Jeremiah 1:7-8)**.

You and I read that and think, "Wait a minute. The Lord is sending the young prophet to His people. Why should he be afraid? This is blessed work, right?" Oh, yeah. It really is in a hundred ways. But in other ways…

God went on, *"They will fight against you, but they shall not prevail against you, for I am with you to deliver you."*

I hate that. You go to bring God's message of love to His people and some of them – not all, thankfully – instead of welcoming you, organize a lynching party.

In his book *Beyond Band of Brothers*, Major Dick Winters tells his side of the story of Easy Company, the men of the 101st Airborne who stormed Normandy and fought their way into Germany. Anyone interested in leadership will find a hundred lessons and that many illustrations, both positive and negative.

But there is one overriding difference in leadership in the Kingdom of God – that is, the Lord's church – and on the battlefield. Once Dick Warren was put in charge of his battalion, he selected his own leaders. He moved people around as he saw fit. He decided on the basis of the character, talents, and abilities of the individuals and cared little how they felt about it, how it suited their career plans, or whether they liked him.

In the church, we're working with volunteers. Many seem to feel they have the God-given right to choose which of the acts of the pastors they will support, which of the sermons they will receive, and in which of his ministries they will participate.

That gets old really quickly. The young pastor blows into this ministry full of vigor and vitality, possessed of a vision for changing the world, having revival, and transforming the church. Then he runs into the reality of old wineskins filled with the ancient bubbly: "We've never done it that way before." "That's not how things get done around here." "Slow down, preacher. We need to run this by Deacon Whoever and Sister Know-it-all."

I've been blessed to mentor several young ministers, i.e., Jimmy Toney, who I baptized at age 13, (I still have a file of letters he sent to me as a child and teenager) who now pastors in Gainesville, Florida. Another minister, Chad Batson – I've pastored him since he was a child, and he now pastors a church in Trumann, Arkansas as well as Everett Loper, pastor in Cleveland, Mississippi. I also have had the joy of mentoring my sons, Devonn and Damon, who are involved working for God in their church and so many others. I've counseled them with these words, "Boys, the Lord has put a delicate balance in His church. He has put just enough headstrong, ornery members to keep you humble. And He has put just enough sweet, godly saints to keep you from quitting."

Thank God for those who keep us from quitting!

These are the ones who do their work well without complaining. They do not stop to look around to see if someone is receiving accolades that should be coming their way instead. They do not expect nor demand nor even desire recognition or reward except from the Heavenly Father Himself.

These are low-maintenance, high-return members. Churches run on them the way a Hummer thrives on high-octane petrol. These are the ones who make a preacher want to give his best, stay in the trenches, and try it again another day.

Thank God for church members who are Christ-like, who take their ministry seriously, and who live to serve the Lord by serving people.

If anyone on earth knows the joys and headaches of life in the pastorium, it's the preacher's kids. Our sons, Devonn and Damon, saw it all up close and personal. Because of their personal convictions, the ministry will not become the targets of sniper fire from these young men. They have loved all their pastors, supported them, and prayed for them for a lot of good reasons, but primarily because they know how special the minister and his family are and how vulnerable they are to attack.

I've witnessed the oddest thing. Once in a while someone will tell me something helpful, encouraging, affirming or endearing that they did for their pastor. I find myself warming on the inside, as though they had done it for me. My spirit is taking that personally. It's an odd reaction, and I suppose it indicates the solid bonding of my heart with these men of the Lord.

But if a poor servant like me feels that way, how much more the Heavenly Father? He takes personally the slights and arrows slung toward the shepherd whom He sends to feed and lead the flock. Likewise, He watches as someone blesses the pastor with a hug, a few extra dollars, a casserole, a book, or a note of encouragement and records it in Heaven as though the acts were done for God Himself.

What a precious thing that we can bless the Lord by the way we treat one another, particularly the shepherd He sends to us.

Amen.

Be encouraged friend! Who else would enjoy hearing this story today?

Chapter Fifteen

A Voice in the Wilderness

"In the beginning of the gospel of Jesus Christ, the Son of God; As it is written in the prophets, Behold, I send my messenger before thy face, which shall prepare thy way before thee. The voice of one crying in the wilderness, Prepare ye the way of the Lord, make his paths straight."

Mark 1:1-3

Do you recognize the name Susan Bennett? Many of you hear her voice every day. Let me acquaint you with her. Susan was born in Clinton, NY in 1948. She is 5'5" tall and weighs 118 pounds.

Susan earned the nickname Tillie in 1974 when she became the voice for the First National Bank of Atlanta's "Tillie the All-Time Teller" which is now what we call an ATM (All Time Machine).

Tillie went on to record messages for the public address system in all Delta Airline Terminals worldwide, as well as voicing e-learning software and GPS navigation software and telephone systems. Bennett's voice has also been used in numerous local and national television advertisements such as Ford, Coca-Cola, Fisher-Price, McDonald's, The Home Depot, Goodyear, Visa, Macy's, Hot Pockets, Club Med and Cartoon Network, among others.

In June 2005, the software company Scan-Soft was looking for someone to be the voice for a database project involving speech construction. Scan-Soft reached out to GM Voices and picked Bennett, who happened to be present when the scheduled voice-over artist was absent. She worked in a home recording booth for the entire month of July 2005, more than four hours each day, reading phrases and sentences. The recordings were then concatenated into the various words, sentences and paragraphs used in the **S**peech **I**nterpretation and **R**ecognition **I**nterface better known as Siri.

Siri is a computer program that works as an intelligent personal assistant and knowledge navigator. The feature uses a natural language user interface to answer questions, make recommendations and perform actions by delegating requests to a set of Web services.

So, someone has been talking to you, answering your questions, giving you directions and until now, just now, you have no idea who she is. IMAGINE! Millions hear her voice everyday but don't know who she is.

Have you ever thought about the significance of the human voice?

The power of the voice. Some of you had parents who could let you know that you had done wrong – just by how they said your name. (David, or David Devonn Tipton, Jr.)

In Emily Bronte's classic book *Jane Eyre*, Mr. Rochester is a disabled blind man who is left alone after his mentally deranged wife sets fire to and destroys their house. His child's former governess, Jane finally approaches him, Mr. Rochester knows her immediately, even though he cannot see her. He says, "This is her voice."

Voices – voices – there are so many voices.

Many years ago, I lived in Louisiana and became personal friends with Bill Tilley, the District Attorney of Vernon Parish. On many Monday mornings, I would drop by for a quick cup of coffee and a brief hello. The District Attorney was like me; he enjoyed pulling pranks. And we often pulled pranks on each other. On this one particular day, I pulled up in front of the courthouse. There was a car parked on the corner behind me with three of four spaces open between. So, I pulled all the way forward to the front car and then backed down to the car in front; when I was ready to leave, it would be an easy pull out. Well, when I got out of the car to walk across the street, I heard this voice that said, "Sir, will you please move your car?" I thought to myself, this is a joke. So, I ignored it and kept walking. Then I heard it again, "Sir, I am asking you to move your car." I took a quick glance upstairs at the courthouse, looked around, but continued to walk. This time, the plea was more demanding. "Sir! Please move your car! I am under your vehicle!" Well, my curiosity got the best of me. I walked back across the street, knelt down and looked under my car. And there was a hardhat sticking out of a manhole just beneath my fuel tank.

Voices!

I knew a man in DeFuniak Springs, Florida named Buford Senerfitt who had the rare ability of throwing his voice. He used that ability to have lots of fun tricking people. He told me when he was a young man following the great depression, he had a little fun with this little black boy walking down the lane one day. During those days, most everybody would cook and eat a terrapin. So, Mr. Senerfitt placed this terrapin in the middle of the lane and hid behind a bush. This little hungry boy sees the terrapin and rushes over, picks him up and says to the turtle, "I am going to eat you tonight." And the terrapin spoke back to him and said, "What is you gonna do to me?" The little boy quickly placed him back on the ground and said, "I am gonna put you right back where I gotcha."

Voices – you never know where they come from. Jesus said, "*My sheep know my voice…*"

Voices are so important in our lives. We are living in a wilderness – you need a voice in your life! You need a pastor to speak into your life when you are going through the wilderness.

When people come to our church, what do you think they come to see? Here is the secret to a strong Apostolic Church. They don't come to see our building, our clothes or our cars. They come to hear from God. They come to see something supernatural. They come to see and hear the life-changing power of the Spirit of God.

We need a voice in our life – God speaks to His people!

God has spoken to His people from the very beginning.

"And they heard the voice of the Lord God walking in the garden in the cool of the day: and Adam and his wife hid themselves from the presence of the Lord God amongst the trees of the garden."

Genesis 3:8

God spoke to His people through the prophets:

"God, who at sundry times and in divers manners spake in time past unto the fathers by the prophets,"

Hebrews 1:1

The issue in biblical times and today is this: Can you hear what God is saying? God is certainly speaking:

"He that hath an ear, let him hear what the Spirit saith unto the churches; He that overcometh shall not be hurt of the second death."

Revelation 2:11

"Howbeit when he, the Spirit of truth is come, he will guide you into all truth: for he shall not speak of himself; but whatsoever he shall hear, that shall he speak: and he will shew you things to come."

John 16:13

We need to get ahold of God like never before because He is speaking a vital message in these last days. He is looking for someone to deliver a timely, life-changing Word.

God has given you a pastor.

"And I will give you pastors according to mine heart, which shall feed you with knowledge and understanding."
Jeremiah 16:13

"Surely the Lord God will do nothing, but he revealeth his secret unto his servants the prophets."
Amos 3:7

"The secret things belong unto the Lord our God: but those things which are revealed belong unto us and to our children forever, that we may do all the words of this law."
Deuteronomy 29:29

We Need A Word From God!

"How then shall they call on him in whom they have not believed? and how shall they believe in him of whom they have not heard? and how shall they hear without a preacher?"
Romans 10:14

A Commentary on Preaching

Preaching is difficult, if not impossible, to define. We all know what it is not, or at least, what it should not be.

Whatever it involves, preaching is the means by which God chose to save them that believe. The man who stands before an assemblage of eternal souls with a Bible before him must ever remember the awesome responsibility that is his. Those who hear him need the message, clear and ungarbled.

Eternity hangs in the balance. Therefore, preaching must be more than educational discourses or theological lectures. It must reach the heart! It must make an impression and that impression must be something of worth. Preaching is, or should be, a mixture of the message and messenger, in which the messenger is, for the most part, unnoticed. Only the deepest sincerity in the preacher can accomplish that; simulated sincerity won't! The true message of God needs no support from cheap showmanship.

Only the false and ugly needs and begs the ornament of human sensationalism. We must steep ourselves in the scripture and literally "preach the Word." People cannot live long on a diet of syrup compliments or watered-down theology. People need the Word of Life. A well-rounded diet of sound, seasoned, stimulating scripture-based preaching will keep God's flock healthy. Never has the church needed preaching as it does today. It needs preachers who are aware of the magnitude of the matter. Every time the pulpit is occupied, it must count! The Word must be preached! Doctrine must be preached! Love must be preached! Holiness and Righteousness must be preached! Preach the Word! Preach! Pray for Preachers! (anon)

Without a word from God, without the energizing breath of the Holy Ghost, we are only a mere form of what we can be.

This is similar to the valley of dry bones Ezekiel saw. Before the prophet lay a potential army, but without the Word of the Lord, they were merely a form of what they could have been.

There are some amazing principles we can learn from Ezekiel 37:1-9:

1 The hand of the Lord was upon me, and carried me out in the spirit of the Lord, and set me down in the midst of the valley which was full of bones. **(You must confess that you are merely a form of what you could be. The valley was "full of bones").**

2 *And caused me to pass them round about: and, behold, there were very many in the open valley; and lo, they were very dry.* **(Very dry)**

3 *And he said unto me, Son of man, can these bones live? And I answered, O Lord God, thou knowest.*

The structure of an army was just waiting for God's command.

You must hear the Word of the Lord!

4 *Again he said unto me, Prophesy upon these bones, and say unto them, O ye dry bones hear the word of the Lord.*

The anointing only falls upon Truth. The Word brings the Truth, which ultimately makes us free.

"And ye shall know the truth, and the truth shall make you free."
John 8:32

The Word will bring about change. The dry bones heard and were quickened.

Then they heard their potential. They knew they were not complete at this stage.

5 *Thus saith the Lord God unto these bones; Behold, I will cause breath to enter into you, and ye shall live:*

6 *And I will lay sinews upon you, and will bring up flesh upon you, and cover you with skin, and put breath in you, and ye shall live; and ye shall know that I am the Lord.*

7 *So I prophesied as I was commanded: and as I prophesied, there was a noise, and behold a shaking, and the bones came together, bone to his bone.*

The Word brought a whole lot of shaking. We need to be shaken out of our complacency. As the broken pieces began to come together, they began to make some noise. God will speak to your broken and shattered dreams.

"Dem Dry Bones" is a well-known spiritual song. The melody was composed by African American author and songwriter James Weldon John (1871-1938).

Ezekiel connected dem dry bones, Ezekiel connected dem dry bones, Ezekiel in the Valley of Dry Bones, Now hear the word of the Lord.

Toe bone connected to the foot bone
Foot bone connected to the heel bone
Heel bone connected to the ankle bone
Ankle bone connected to the shin bone
Shin bone connected to the knee bone
Knee bone connected to the thigh bone
Thigh bone connected to the hip bone
Hip bone connected to the backbone
Backbone connected to the shoulder bone
Shoulder bone connected to the neck bone
Neck bone connected to the head bone
Now hear the Word of the Lord.

Dem bones, dem bones gonna walk around
Dem bones, dem bones gonna walk around
Dem bones, dem bones gonna walk around
Now hear the Word of the Lord.

What needs to happen when some things are coming together yet you still don't have a complete victory? You keep preaching! Prophesy again!

9 *Then said he unto me, Prophesy unto the wind, prophesy, son of man, and say to the wind, Thus saith the Lord God; Come from the four winds, O breath, and breathe upon these slain, that they may live.*

The potential was realized as the Word brought about the rain.

The Word came from the four corners of the earth. That tells me there isn't an area that God cannot fill with the Holy Ghost. Your past, your childhood, your feeling of inferiority, your wounds, your loneliness. The Holy Ghost can fill you from the North, South, East and West. *God's gonna send revival to this land... from the North, the South, the East and the West. God's gonna send revival to this land.*

Initially the pile of bleached bones had potential that Ezekiel could not see. No matter what others say, God sees incredible potential in this church, in you. Within you is an army. We need a voice in our lives, a voice in the wilderness!

Healing, brokenness – preacher preach!

Be encouraged friend! Who else would enjoy hearing this story today?

Chapter Sixteen

Jumpin' Cross-ties

"Fear will shout about who you were; love will whisper about who we are becoming. Listen to the truest voice, not the loudest one."

Bob Goff

24 *There be four things which are little upon the earth, but they are exceeding wise:*
25 *The ants are a people not strong, yet they prepare their meat in the summer,*
26 *The conies are but a feeble folk, yet make they their houses in the rocks;*
27 *The locusts have no king, yet they go forth all of them by bands;*
28 *The spider taketh hold with her hands, and is in kings' palaces.*

Proverbs 30:24-28

The ants are not strong but prepare for winter by working together. If one ant can't lift the crumb and take it back to the colony, it will signal for help to get the overwhelming task complete.

The conies (that's not a hotdog from Sonic) – are always having to look out for predators. Yet they build their homes in the most difficult place, the rocks.

The locusts don't have a king. They don't have a leader. Yet they can devastate an entire crop overnight.

The tiny insignificant spider will not let anything stop her from getting into the king's house. She works with her little hands. With determination she finds entry into the palace.

Overcoming difficulties and accepting challenges is a vital part of the journey of faith.

I remember the first time that I was laughed at. Before I tell the story, I must qualify. My mother made sure that our clothes were clean, and our hair was combed before we went out the door. I had new clothes any time I needed them. However, new clothes made me itch! Nothing like a pair of worn jeans, with patches and an old pair of socks. My mom would have nearly died if she knew I went to school with a hole in one of my socks!

My first-grade class was playing drop the handkerchief during recess. Someone finally dropped the handkerchief in my hand. I took off like greased lightning and when I did – one of my shoes came off. Yes, the shoe on the foot that had a hole in the sock. All my classmates started laughing. But as I recall, it didn't seem to bother me. I turned around, raced back to grab my shoe, slipped it back on my foot and got back in the game.

That's life – that's what people say, shot down in April, back up in May (Sung by Frank Sinatra).

I don't think I'm unique in that regard. Everyone has setbacks, difficulties, and obstacles to overcome.

My wife and I married on March 11, 1978. Her sweet mother had been diagnosed with cancer, but thankfully was well enough to attend our wedding in West Point, Mississippi. I was the proud owner of a Buick Electra 225, a two door, sharp ride! It had a landau top, Buick mags and corduroy 60/40 seats. However, just shortly after we were married, the engine blew. What good is a nice-looking vehicle with a bad engine? At this time, I didn't want to tell anyone about my struggles.

The Air Force was transferring my brother-in-law, Bobby Byram and his family to Spain. He asked if they could store some of their belongings in our utility shed. As I looked through that shed, there was a Honda 50cc minibike.

I retrieved it from the shed and began using that as my means of transportation back and forth from work. The railroad track that ran behind my house also went to the factory where I was employed. So, I would put on my metatarsal boots, safety glasses with side-shields and a hard hat and jump cross-ties for nearly three miles. You are talking about a sight! I am sure that I looked like some kind of alien sitting on something that was way too small for an adult.

It is not a joy ride in an amusement park to jump cross-ties. While I was increasing and decreasing the throttle, my heart was so broken and tears were flowing. I began to ask God, "Why is this happening to us?"

My wife played the piano in church, and I was the worship leader and youth teacher. We paid our tithes and offerings. We were faithful to church. I was saying, "God I am giving you my best, and this just isn't fair." I continued the washboard effect down the railroad track. It seemed that all of a sudden, peace came over me, and God began speaking to my heart. This warm impression came over me, and it communicated to my spirit. "Son, everything is going to be all right. One day you will be able to tell the story of how you overcame. You will testify and witness to someone who will be experiencing pain and difficulties." I want to say that it got better. But hold on, it's going to get a little bumpier.

My wife got very sick. I had to borrow a vehicle (a Buick) to take her to the emergency room. They admitted her into Lowndes County Hospital. While she was in the hospital, one morning the phone rang and it was my brother-in-law, Bobby. He said, "Are you near Gwen?"

I said, "Yes."

"Don't react, but I'm calling to let you know her mom just passed."

I had the difficult job of telling Gwen. I found the doctor who reluctantly discharged her so we could go pack and drive to Paragould, Arkansas. About halfway between Columbus and West Point, the Buick overheated, blew a head gasket, and there my sick wife and I sat on the side of the road bewildered!! I hate Buicks to this day! I've told this story, and I've preached it many times. Andre Crouch wrote the song, but I've lived it. *"I've got confidence, God is gonna see me through. No matter what the case may be..."*

This story happened several years before I started preaching. But it leads me to include this testimony of God's healing power.

I was working as a technician in a metallurgical laboratory. Making good money, excellent insurance benefits, ambient temperature year-round in the laboratory while in the factory, there was no heat or air conditioning.

Our oldest son Devonn was born with asthma. On many occasions we would rush him to the emergency room where they would put him under an oxygen tent. One night, I remember us loading him into our four-door Vette (Chevette) and the nurse rushing out to the vehicle to retrieve him from my wife's arms. He was turning blue around his lips and eyes, and he was gasping for breath. With good insurance, it was the first thing to do.

However, the Lord was dealing with me about preaching. So, I went and talked to my pastor. In his wisdom, he told me to take a six-week sabbatical and not quit my job. He was going to line me up with some revivals. I remember returning from Largo, Florida pulling a 19-foot travel trailer that my wife looked over at me with concern and said, "If we do this and go on the road, what's going to happen if Devonn has an asthma attack and we're out here with no insurance and no money?"

We looked at each other and agreed if our pastor gave us his blessing, then we would need to trust God. I went back to work, turned in my two weeks' notice, and we hit the field two weeks later! Giving thanks and glory to God – Devonn is now 40 years old and has never had another asthma attack!

Dear discouraged friend, it may get bumpy, but I promise you, it will get better. Keep going forward, that's where your destiny is!

The diving spider is a very unique little creature. It lives and breathes fresh air just beneath the surface of the water. It spreads a huge bubble of fresh air. When the air is lost, the diving spider ascends right to the top without wasting time and grabs another breath of fresh air… creates another bubble and goes right back down into the depths of the hostile environment.

You and I live in a culture today that spends every day of life trying to puncture this experience, this freshness and this power that we love, enjoy and live in.

And every once in a while, our spiritual world is penetrated and something or someone bursts our bubble; but that's when we come right back to the house of God and create another bubble of spirituality; we sing a song, pray a prayer, and we are handed a sword and bread from the man of God who ministers to us through the Word of God. Then we go right back into a hostile environment.

That's why the Bible said: *"…greater is he that is in you, than he that is in the world."*

Let me remind you: Circumstances can't kill your dream; criticism can't kill your dream, and outside forces are not authorized to kill your dream. The Devil is not authorized to kill your dream.

I started out and I'm going to finish this race I have begun.

Be encouraged friend! Who else would enjoy hearing this story today?

Note: Sketch by Gene Lyons. I promised him if I ever wrote a book that I would include his drawing.

Chapter Seventeen

He's My Brother!

"A friend loveth at all times, and a brother is born for adversity."

Proverbs 17:17

Connectivity, closeness and commitment. The world we live in is desperate for it. The church, now more than ever, needs to show it so that it can draw the rest of the world to Jesus Christ.

After all, this was His prayer… That we would be one. As for the church, we are called to be the bride of Christ… We are family. We must always stick together. How can we help others if we don't first determine in our heart and mind to stick together? I believe in Unity with everything that is within me. It has been with me ever since I was a child. There are moments that are so vivid in my mind.

I remember sitting in my classroom with my classmates. Our teacher announced that she would have to be out of class for a little while and that she was assigning us some work to do to keep us busy. She was appointing (let's just call him John*) to sit at her desk and take names of anyone who talked. She had barely gotten out of the room when John looked at me and said, "David, I'm giving you a zero."

I said, "Why? I wasn't talking."

He replied, "Just because I want to."

I told him, "You better erase the zero by my name."

He refused, so, I went up to the desk, took the pencil out of his hand, turned the roll book around and erased the zero.

He said, "Oh, that means you want to fight, don't you?" He halfway stood up and challenged me and said, "Where do you want to meet after school?" I told him the golf course would be fine.

As soon as school was out, I went straight to my brother and told him what was going on. We set out walking the three or four blocks over to the golf course. When we turned the corner, we were shocked to see that John had a fan club. He had gone around the school and told everybody to come to the fight. They were all in a circle, and John was standing in the middle. My brother and I figured out right quick like that it was he and I against the world.

So, I just walked up and pushed my way between classmates and continued to walk toward John while my brother Steve joined the circle. John was just standing there, and I knew that whatever I did, I would have to do it quickly. So, I just walked straight up to him and before he knew what hit him, I threw my now famous left jab and knocked him on the ground. I then jumped on top of him and began to rearrange his face.

Well, John's girlfriend, (we'll just call her Jane*) was standing in the circle, couldn't just stand there and watch her boyfriend get whipped. So, she jumped on, dug her fingernails into and down my back.

Steve was standing there watching a fair fight until Jane attacked his brother. So, Steve stepped up and caught her under the chin and knocked her backwards. Well, there was John lying one way flat on his back and at his feet was Jane lying horizontally. My brother and I pushed our way back through the casual observers and walked home.

David pushing Steve,
1959

You know what felt good that day? It wasn't that I defeated John. It was that my brother fought for me. My brother stood with me.

All these years later, I still feel that way. Sometimes the greatest victories are experienced when I have had a spiritual brother with me. Just knowing that he had my back… that we were UNITED in the cause, was strength to me.

So, when life comes against us and tries to keep us down and pull us away from doing the work God has called us to do… it is up to all of us to fight for each other. We are family. Families must be UNITED. No matter what, you're my brother and my sister. United there is nothing that we cannot accomplish.[2]

Be encouraged friend! Who else would enjoy hearing this story today?

---

[2] *Names changed to protect the defeated.*

Chapter Eighteen

Call Home

"The Lord is nigh unto all them that call upon him, to all that call upon him in truth."

Psalms 145:18

There was a minister in a certain church who would call the children down to the front of the church every Sunday and tell them a story. One time, he brought a telephone to illustrate the idea of prayer. He said, "Now kids, you know how you can talk to people on the telephone, but you can't see them on the other end of the line? But you know they are there?" The children nodded yes. He said, "Well, talking to God is just like talking on the telephone. He's on the other end of the line even though you can't see Him, and He's listening."

About that time a little boy piped up and said, "What's his number?"

I recently spotted a bumper sticker that made the poignant plea: *"You are a child of God. Please call home."*

Who hasn't felt the need to 'call home' at different points in our lives? Phoning home puts us in touch with a place where we feel the safest, the most loved, and the most familiar.

Can you remember your first phone number? I can! Ours was 785-2389. I've called that number many times for many reasons.

When I was old enough to drive, my parents set a weekday curfew of 10 pm and Friday and Saturdays were 11 pm.

I recall one weeknight when I had just turned sixteen. I think it was after mid-week service, and I was taking my girlfriend (the lovely, beautiful Gwenda Hayes) home to Tyndall Air Force Base. I was driving my 1973 Ford Maverick. I had a flat tire around 9:30 pm. There was no way that I could change the tire, drive to the base and then be home by my 10 pm curfew. I pulled into a Hardee's parking lot, rushed over to the phone booth and slid a dime in. I dialed 785-2389, and my dad answered. I explained my situation. By 10:15, I was home having changed the tire, dropped my sweetheart off, and made it in record time!

I left home when I was seventeen years old. I moved over four hundred miles away - from Panama City, Florida to West Point, Mississippi. I took a job as a produce manager at Sunflower.

I was an adult! A big boy! However, one day I had this overwhelming, all-consuming, homesick feeling. I was missing home. I was REALLY missing mom and dad.

It became too much for me. I walked out of the store to the pay phone mounted on the brick wall, next to the coke machine. I didn't have any money, so I picked up the receiver and dialed 0.

The Operator answered, "May I help you?" I said, "Yes ma'am, I'd like to place a collect call to David or Faye Tipton."

I can't tell you how I relieved I was to hear my parents' 'yes'. Of course, I never doubted that they would take my call.

This big ol' boy began to cry. I said, "Mom and Dad, I sure am missing you. I just wanted to hear your voice again. Mom, I sure wish I could sit at your table and eat your homemade biscuits. Dad, you don't know how much I'd love to see you."

Not only was I overjoyed to hear their voices on the other end of the line, but they were also just as happy to hear mine.

I'm so glad that we don't need money or a pedigree. We don't even have to have a certain last name. Our Father awaits our call. He wants to hear our voice. He wants to tell us how much He loves us.

Reminds me of the song, "Reach out and touch the Lord." Why don't you reach out and call home? He's waiting!

Be encouraged friend! Who else would enjoy hearing this story today?

Chapter Nineteen

Faith, Freedom & Politics

The Bible teaches us to do everything possible to be good citizens and to be involved for the betterment of our society. In Jeremiah 29:7 (NIV), God tells us to *"seek the peace and prosperity of the city to which I have carried you… because if it prospers, you too will prosper."*

Exercising our Christian citizenship is crucial in today's world if we want to make our witness, knowledge, and influence count. The dedicated men and women of the Church have a glorious opportunity in this day and time to employ Christian values and models to the political structure.

I have recently had the pleasure of writing the book **Faith, Freedom & Politics**. I am truly a believer that a part of being a good citizen is being genuinely involved with the political life of nation, state, and community.

Because of this, I have had the honor of attending political rallies, functions and events. I have had the pleasure of praying over governors and presidents. I count many of Mississippi leaders as well as some national leaders as friends.

I had the privilege of praying over our Mississippi rally in Southaven, Mississippi for President Trump in 2018.

Trump Rally Prayer – 2018

Father, we are here tonight at a great tipping point in our national history. We come here, for just a brief moment, to stop the world. We pause collectively, and with one voice, ask you to bless our President as he works diligently to Make America Great Again. Grant him strength that is equal to the weight of his office and wisdom to lead his nation forward.

We are thankful that we live in a country that provides us with the freedom to express our beliefs and elect leaders who represent those beliefs. We are thankful for leaders who still stop to seek your guidance and possess a faith that continues to inform their politics.

God, we thank you for our President, Donald Trump. We lift him up to you and trust you are able to do above and beyond what we can ask or think. Together, in this place, we dedicate ourselves and the future of America to you.

Because of your blessings, our greatest days are yet to come. You have great plans for us. Your Word tells us in the book of Jeremiah: *"I know the plans I have for you, plans to prosper you and not to harm you, plans to give you hope and a future. Then you will call upon me and come and pray to me, and I will listen to you. You will seek me and find me when you seek me with all your heart."* This is what we do here tonight.

Finally, Lord, we thank you for your assurance that true freedom comes, not from the generosity of the state, but from your hand alone. Your word assures us that the freedom You give can never be taken away. No matter what trials come our way, we can stand upon your promise that no weapon formed against us shall prosper.

In the words of Sir Francis Drake: we ask You to: "Push back the horizons of our hopes, and to look to the future in strength, courage, hope, and love." Let the coming years of this administration be a time where all the great things that we've imagined for America becomes a reality.

In Jesus' Name we pray, and it is so.

Photo Submitted

Dinner guests at mansion ...

Rev. David Tipton and his sons, Damon and Devonn were recent dinner guests of Gov. Kirk Fordice at the Governor Mansion.

Mississippi Governor Phil Bryant
& Chief Justice Randolph

Mississippi Governor
& RNC Chairman Haley Barbour

Mississippi Governor
Phil Bryant

British Parliament
Nigel Farage

Mississippi Governor and Mrs. Tate Reeves

Alabama State Senator
& Former Attorney General Jeff Sessions

To my friend David Tipton with admiration.
Robert Wicker

Mississippi State Senator Roger Wicker
Mississippi District UPC Political Liaison Ron Matis

Student Religious Liberties Act
Bill Signing with Governor Phil Bryant

Retired Commander of Israeli
Northern Defense Elliot Chodoff

Labor Secretary Wilbur Ross

Reverend Franklin Graham

Transportation Commissioner Willie Simmons
& Senator John Horhn

Family Research Council President Tony Perkins

Georgia Senator David Perdue

Be encouraged friend! Who else would enjoy hearing this story today?

Chapter Twenty

Author & Finisher

"According as he hath chosen us in him before the foundation of the world, that we should be holy and without blame before him in love: Having predestinated us unto the adoption of children by Jesus Christ to himself, according to the good pleasure of his will."

Ephesians 1:4-5 KJV

"Being confident of this very thing, that he which hath begun a good work in you will perform it until the day of Jesus Christ:"

Philippians 1:6 KJV

"Looking unto Jesus the author and finisher of our faith; who for the joy that was set before him endured the cross, despising the shame, and is set down at the right hand of the throne of God."

Hebrews 12:2

The Psalmist in song number 139 wrote:

You created every part of me;
You put me together in my mother's womb.
I praise you because you are to be feared;
All you do is strange and wonderful,
I know it with all my heart.
When my bones were being formed,
Carefully put together in my mother's womb,
When I was growing there in secret,
You knew that I was there.
You saw me before I was born.

I didn't know it until I researched it, but most anyone would think that when movies are made, the directors and actors start at the first scene and continue until the last scene is shot. Not so.

Many times, the last scene or a scene in the middle of the movie is shot first. Then the first scenes are filmed so they work into the latter scenes. In many cases, the very beginning of the movie is the last part filmed. The movie can be produced in this way because everyone is working from a script that gives them the whole story, beginning to end.

From the moment of your birth until this very moment, God has been working behind the scenes.

He's the finisher! My purpose in life is not wrapped up in fulfilling this world's expectations of me. My future, my destiny, my reason for living is derived from the ONE who gave me life.

As a child, I grew up with an unhealthy fear that my dad would get killed while driving intoxicated. On more than one occasion, he would decide to stay behind at the bar where he and his buddies were drinking and playing pool. Finding later the car he came in would leave to go to another bar and the passengers would be killed or injured. I remember when I was thirteen or fourteen years old, during pre-service prayer, I was so disturbed that I went into a small room alone and wept in the dark.

My pastor came in and asked what was wrong. I told him that I was afraid my dad was going to die because of his lifestyle. He kindly, yet sternly told me that was a spirit of fear and not from God. I knew this to be true, but it was difficult to shake.

Years go by. It is in the 1980's. I am now pastoring in Georgetown, Louisiana, and one night I had a terrible nightmare. Horrid scenes began to unfold. Beginning with

154

receiving a phone call informing me my dad was dying. If I wanted to see him before his death, I must come quickly.

In this dream, I rushed to the neighborhood where my parents resided. As I approached from a block away, I could not get to my parents' house for the cars that were parked up and down both sides of the street. I parked my vehicle and could see the horror in my own face as I ran down the street. As I passed each car, there were these demonic beings sitting inside their vehicles or leaning on the fenders and mockingly laughing, giving me a look; they were delighted to inform me that my dad had died. They said, "Ha! Ha! You were the only one not there." I did get to the front porch only to see my dad had slumped down against the wall where he squatted every day to smoke his cigarette. And there he was with my family gathered around, clasping a cigarette between his fingers and dead.

The demonic forces seem to take such joy in how it all ended.

I had not told anyone about my troubling dream. A few days later, Brother and Sister Fred Scott, a wonderful couple I pastored, approached me after service and said to me, "The Lord has laid it on our heart to take you to Florida to see your parents. We will pick you up on Monday morning in our motorhome and drop you off at your parents and come back by later in the week to take you back home." They had no idea of the serious urge I had to go check on my dad.

While there one evening, dad and I were out on the front porch and I shared the horrific dream with him. The color seemed to have left his face, and he had this unusual look on his face as he said, "Have you told this to your mother?"

I said, "No sir, that's up to you. This is between you, God, and mom."

In 2004, dad got very sick while visiting us in Grenada. He really wanted to go home, back to Panama City, so he could be in his own bed, but he was just too sick. He emerged out of the bedroom one morning and told mom not to worry about him. He had been talking to God and felt like he had fixed everything. Finally, I persuaded him to let me take him to the hospital in Oxford. After a chest x-ray, they admitted him. The doctor told my brothers and me that dad would never leave the hospital alive; he was in the last stage of lung cancer.

He seemed to improve and was in good spirits. This was the last week of July 2004. I would go back and forth to check on him. However, on this particular night, after company from other family members and visiting hours were over, I went to his bedside, hugged him and told him I was leaving and would return the following day to check on him.

I walked half-way across the room, and he said, "Son, you know you're a sleepy-headed driver. You stay awake and watch them deer."

I said, "Okay, dad. I love you." I got to the door and was about to say goodbye for the third time when all of a sudden, I had an unexplainable urge come over me.

In a flash I said, "I've changed my mind. I am not going anywhere. I am going to sit down right here in this chair and spend the night with you." He didn't say one thing about me going on home. He seemed to like the idea that I was staying the night. He was in good spirits, wasn't struggling and seemed peaceful.

He said, "Son, now go ahead and get some sleep, I'm going to be alright."

From 9 pm to 5 am on August 4, 2004, I would wake up in intervals of fifteen to thirty minutes, and as I opened my eyes each time, his eyes would open, staring right down at me with a look I always wanted to see. A countenance of peace,

156

a look of acceptance, a look that was saying, "Son, I am proud of you." And each time he would say, "Son, I am fine. Go on back to sleep, I'll be alright. I love you."

Then I would say, "I love you too, dad!" At 5 am, I was privileged to be present when he transitioned from this life to the next.

It is not our prerogative to put anyone anywhere in eternity. That is left up to our Savior and Judge. But I do know that Satan's plans were for the last paragraph of the last chapter to end in a way that would have been difficult to deal with. His plans were thwarted. The page was ripped out, and mercy rewrote my dad's life. Thank you, Jesus! You started with the end in mind.

The Pen Remains in the Author's Hand

Mike Manuel

Jesus Christ is the Author and the finisher of faith.
What he started in your life; He will complete.
So, don't worry about tomorrow
Just live for God today.
And remember, He controls your fate
And your happy ending is on its way

Cause the pen is still in the Author's hand.
It's not over… You haven't reached the end.

A good author never lets his hero die,
And you know the good guys always win.
Cause the pen remains – in the Author's hand.

Like a hero in a story book
You'll have your ups and downs.
And who knows what awaits you in the next town.
So, sit tall in the saddle
Through each chapter of your life
And face every battle with a grin

Cause there's no colt faster than the Author's pen.

Remember this:

"Remember the former things, those of long ago; I am God, and there is no other; I am God, and there is none like me. I make known the end from the beginning, from ancient times, what is still to come. I say, 'My purpose will stand, and I will do all I please. 'From the east I summon a bird of prey, from a far-off land, a man to fulfill my purpose. What I have said, that I will bring about; what I have planned, that I will do."

Isaiah 46:9-11 (NIV)

Be encouraged friend! Who else would enjoy hearing this story today?

Chapter Twenty-One

Let God

On August 26, 2019, I was diagnosed with a rare cancer called Urachal Adeno Carcinoma. I was admitted to the hospital on September 5th for surgery to remove a tumor and cancerous tissue. A partial cystectomy was performed, and several lymph nodes were removed. The cancer cells were found in the bladder wall, my vascular system, and in a few lymph nodes. The incision required twenty-seven staples to close. The pathology report gave devastating news. After several days in the hospital, I was discharged with the news that in eight weeks following surgery, I was to undergo twelve weeks (intermittently) of chemotherapy treatments that I respectfully declined. After two or three weeks, I recall sitting in my living room recuperating from surgery. Depression slipped into my room, and the window shades of my heart closed.

I felt that I was being attacked from all sides. It seemed I was on the canvas in the middle of a boxing ring and from all four corners of the ring, I was being hit. From one corner, came finances charging, the other corner, my health was being assaulted, my imaginations and emotions were hitting me with the jaw-breaking uppercuts. To top it all off, the transmission in my vehicle went out. Life had me in a full Nelson hold.

In my mind, I began planning my funeral. Who I wanted to speak and sing, etc.

While sitting in my recliner, in a dark room with nothing but a reading lamp over my head, I began to make my complaints known to God.

As I sat there, hooked up to attachments (I felt like a vacuum cleaner with all those attachments) asking God – Why me? I've never smoked, never drank, dipped or chewed tobacco. Why have you allowed me to get cancer? Not only cancer, but a rare, one in a million per year cancer, most medical professionals have never heard of or treated.

After I questioned God and asked Him all the "why's," He began speaking to me similarly as He did Job.

I taught my children to not use the word shut up – but God is God. He can say what he wants to. He told me to shut up!

At times we are tempted to try to explain God. But if God were so easily comprehended in our human understanding, He would not be God. At the other end of the spectrum, God is not so remote as to leave us speechless. He does come to us and will always leave His witness among us.

There comes a time in every one of us when we will begin to doubt God's intention; we doubt His presence; we doubt His provision. In other words, we just don't understand what's going on or how what we are facing can possibly be for our good. How can a loving God, an all-powerful God, an all-knowing God – just stand aside and watch us suffer? Why doesn't God do something about it right now? What's He waiting on? What does He expect of me before the answer will come? God, Where Are YOU? I need you now, not tomorrow, or the next day, but right now! Why can't I get the answer I need today? What are you waiting for?

Those who are suffering from sickness and disease are trying to believe God for their miracle of healing, but for some reason, it just isn't happening – at least not the way we would want it to. God, I know you can, but I don't know IF you will! Those having other kinds of troubles have the same questions too.

None of us doubt we have a God that can do anything. We all know the Word of God promises that all things will work together for our good if we will serve the Lord. But Lord, I'm holding up my end of the deal to the best of my ability; when are you going to move on my behalf?

Am I the only one who has ever thought these things or questioned God? I think not! These thoughts are all part of the human condition.

In Job chapters 38 and 39, we find God asking Job a lot of questions. In those two chapters, we find God asking more questions of a man than anywhere else in the Bible. In those two chapters, there are 59 questions that God asked of Job. The amazing thing is that Job could not answer even one of God's questions.

Why was God asking Job all of these questions?

Job was at the point in his suffering where he was losing confidence in God. He needed a reminder of God's great love and limitless power. He was telling Job – Let me be God!

He gave me three scriptures with these two words: **Let God.**

"Let God arise, let his enemies be scattered: let them also that hate him flee before him."

Psalm 68:1 KJV

Let all those that seek thee rejoice and be glad in thee: and let such as love thy salvation say continually, Let God be magnified."

Psalm 70:4 KJV

"God forbid: yea, Let God be true, but every man a liar; as it is written, That thou mightiest be justified in thy sayings, and mightest overcome when thou art judged."

Romans 3:4 KJV

Let God Arise! - Psalm 68:1
Let God Be Magnified! - Psalm 70:4
Let God Be True! - Romans 3:4

The silence of God ends when our silence begins.

"My hope is built on nothing less than Jesus' blood and righteousness. On Christ the solid rock I stand. All other ground is sinking sand."

Edward Mote

One year later, on September 8, 2020, I write this to give testimony of the healing power of God. With a thankful heart I conclude:

"Thou has turned for me mourning into dancing: thou hast put off my sackcloth, and girded me with gladness; To the end that my glory may sing praise to thee, and not be silent. O Lord my God, I will give thanks unto thee for ever."

Psalm 30:11-12 KJV

Be encouraged friend! Who else would enjoy hearing this story today?

Products by David Tipton

Mississippi Matters
Perspective & Insights from David Tipton
A compilation of articles written to the great people of the
Mississippi District United Pentecostal Church

Gonna Tell Everybody
CD by David & Gwen Tipton
Produced by Kenny Henson

Faith, Freedom & Politics
A guide for a Christian in civic life

Journey of a Lifetime
Personal Stories to stimulate your memory, spark your
imagination and strengthen your faith

Contact Information:
Onward365
David Tipton
P. O. Box 1852
Grenada, MS 38901
www.Onward-365.com

Made in the USA
Middletown, DE
12 December 2021

53961177R00091